Vision Art and History of Art

Peter V. Moak

VISION ART AND HISTORY OF ART
Copyright © 2021 by Peter V. Moak

All rights reserved. No part of this publication may be reproduced, distributed, or transmitted in any form or by any means, including photocopying, recording, or other electronic or mechanical methods, without the prior written permission of the publisher or author, except in the case of brief quotations embodied in critical reviews and certain other noncommercial uses permitted by copyright law.

Although every precaution has been taken to verify the accuracy of the information contained herein, the author and publisher assume no responsibility for any errors or omissions. No liability is assumed for damages that may result from the use of information contained within.

Library of Congress Control Number: 2021918636
ISBN-13: Paperback: 978-1-64749-609-8
E-Pub: 978-1-64749-610-4

Printed in the United States of America

GoTo Publish

GoToPublish LLC
1-888-337-1724
www.gotopublish.com
info@gotopublish.com

VISION, ART AND THE HISTORY OF ART

We stand in awe of nature. It is our source of life and of knowledge and beauty, nature is endless, ambiguous, contradictory and deadly. In contrast a work of art is coherent and finite. It establishes its and our own separate being. For a work of art to accomplish this it must be experienced in a certain way. We have various ways of seeing the world which I call *perspectives*. The particular way we need to see a work of art is one of these. Seeing a work the right way, the way it was seen when it was made is essentials to understanding and appreciation. From time to time, place to place, people to people, culture to culture, nation to nation and artist to artist ways of seeing differ. To understand these ways of seeing which I call *perspectives* I begin with vision.

Vision

We open our eyes and light passes through the lenses and forms pictures on our retinas. Our brain using these tiny reversed inverted images presents us with a life sized three dimensional stable upright lens projected picture, our *visual world*. We exist and act in relation to our visual world and although it is a picture in our head we see it as we should as the real external world. Depth in our interior visual world is represented by diminishing scale which means the visual world is a lens projected picture, a picture of something else, another world, the real outside world. How could it be anything else? I call seeing the interior visual world *vision* and the production of retinal pictures *eyesight*. We see our interior visual world in two basic ways. The first I call *nonaligned* and the second *aligned*. We see nonaligned visual world as separate from us and not around us. Although upright, reversed and apparently much enlarged the nonaligned visual world is similar to the lens projected retinal picture. My eyes as the center of my being stand outside the nonaligned visual world and not in it. When we physically move including just our eyes we extend the nonaligned visual world but do not enter it. We enter the visual world when we become aligned. We do this by imagining a point in the visual world lined up with an imagined point behind our eyes, our *point of view*. These points come into being when we imagine them together, at the same time, with a *line of sight* stretching between them. I call our presence in relation to the visual world, our eyes together with our point of view, our *visual ego* which is now the center of our aligned visual world and the center of out being. [1] When surrounding points in the visual world are seen aligned with the point of view lines and objects in the visual world appear regularized and we can remember them, visualize them and relate them to each other. Changing eye size is called the widening or narrowing of the eyes even though we can not physically change the size of out eyes. However we can seem to do so by imagining points at the corners of our eyes aligned with our point of view and changing the distance between these points. We move our visual ego in and out in the aligned visual world by changing the apparent size of our eyes. When a succeeding object is seen with enlarged it appears farther away. This is one way we separate adjacent objects in depth. I call this *scale reduction*. If we make the apparent size of our eyes smaller than an object we move close to the object and its outlines spread out around us. A small close up visual ego can make a distant object appear life sized a phenomena called *constancy scaling*. If we make our visual ego larger than an object the object is seen across space and spread out in front of us. When I move special continuity between objects is established if before we move we become peripherally aligned to the next object. If we do not do this the next object is seen in a separate space and what I call *disconnected*. Using the above elements of vision: nonalignment, alignment, the visual ego, moving and changing the size of the visual ego, perspective, point of view, lines of sight, the visual ego, peripheral alignment, regularized outlines, memorable shapes, spacial continuity, disconnection and constancy scaling I geometrically order my relationship with my visual world. The relationship that places me at the center of my visual world in ways that compensate for the separateness and diminishing scale of the lens projected nonaligned visual world turning it into a world that more closely resembles the outside physical world. Another ability that influences the way we see the visual world is the power to keep up to four things in our mind at once. The memorable visual units created by the geometric ordering of vision together with the ability to hold one to four units in our mind at the same time enhances the ability to make works of art.

Art

The counter intuitive way I describe vision sounds strange. We are not conscious of the visual procedures, the mental gymnastics I describe. Normal vision seems effortless and automatic. For example we adjust the size of our eyes when we look at television or at the movies without knowing it. Be that as it may my experience that being aware of your visual ego and its actions is necessary when it comes to making pictures, works of art. My experience is that it just so. I find that a *work of art* is a thing made by a human being using an aligned visual ego in a particular way I call the *perspective*. Thus to see a work of art correctly we need to use the same perspective used when it was made. By perspective I do not mean linear perspective, a mechanical drawing procedure that imitates the linear structure and diminishing scale of a lens projected picture and does not require a particular use of the aligned visual ego. I find the right perspective through trial and error. The right perspective makes a work of art look its *aesthetic best* which I find to be a universal resulting from parts that cohere and not a matter of *taste*, taste being an individual or social preference. I find *style* to be a mix of characteristics, perspective being just one. I see things made by animals and our prehistoric relatives the Neanderthals as not depending on an aligned visual ego and not as works of art. For this reason I believe the visual ego is unique to modern human beings, Homo sapiens sapiens. We are a species of artists. I see patterns in perspective use in the history. I see different perspectives following the peopling of the earth which begins in Africa and spreads from there, the Noah's Ark theory. [2] I also see changes in perspective following the evolution of a culture, for example Greek culture from the tenth through the first century B.C. In Europe along with vast social and political changes from the first century B.C. to the twelfth century A.D. and beyond I find perspectives changing. Beginning in Spain in the eleventh century A.D. I find standard perspectives appearing for the emerging nation-states of the West. In the East perspective use remains relatively constant. In the following centuries the perspective used by individual artists becomes important. Since the second half of the twentieth century there has been an effort to escape the bounds created by perspective, the closed world that is a work of art. I find this effort misguided.

Perspectives used in the history of art. (The names are mine.)

Semitic perspective depends on making your visual ego smaller than the object and aligning a point on the object and your point of view. Alignment is continuous if you peripherally align the next object with you point of view before you move. If you do not do this the next object is first seen unaligned and disconnected. I find Semitic perspective in the early art of the people speaking the Semitic languages and so the name. Coming to Western Europe from North Africa in the later middle ages it becomes the most widely used perspective in the Western World.

Oriental perspective uses eyes, visual ego larger than the object. The large Oriental ego places you back from an object which is seen spread out before you and is more planar than the Semitic perspective object. To remain continuously aligned when using Oriental perspective you again see following objects peripherally aligned. I find Oriental perspective common to China, Japan, Korea, South East Asia, the art of Central and South America and that of the native American peoples of North America.

Peripheral Perspective in contrast to Semitic and Oriental perspective that place you before an object peripheral perspective places a small visual ego to the side of an object. Seen in this way the object or a portion thereof is obliquely seen and the composition part by part going left to right. I find peripheral perspective to have a long history beginning with the very early art of peoples speaking the Indo European languages. It is today a characteristic of the art of Indian and of Post Modern architecture.

African Perspective begins with a form seen nonaligned and then seen center aligned with a close by small ego. This procedure isolates shapes that confront you in turn. African perspective is a characteristic of art from sub-Saharan Africa and very early works of art coming from a "path" stretching from sub-Saharan Africa across the Mediterranean to India., South East Asia, Australia and Oceania.

European Perspective is basic to the art of Stone Age Europe, Old Europe, European perspective shapes are first nonaligned and then side aligned with a small ego. As with African perspective disconnection isolates each shapes in turn. European perspective is found in Etruscan and Roman art.

Attic Perspective I find first used in Athens toward the middle of the fifth century BC. Attic perspective forms are seen with a point behind each form aligned to the visual ego that is also a point aligned with a point behind and object. With Attic perspective contours left and right are simultaneously seen in relation to a perpendicular line of sight producing coherent three dimensional forms. I find Attic perspective first used in Athens in about 450 BC.

Hellenic Perspective is a variation on Semitic perspective which uses a somewhat larger ego that so stands moved back from the object resulting in a wider view but a less exact the definition of three dimensional form. Hellenic perspective is used in late fourth century BC Greek art, variously used during the Hellenistic period and first used in 7th century BC Assyrian art.

Renaissance Perspective is based on a central point on the object, rather than behind, aligned to a visual ego that is a point. The Renaissance ego stands further back than Attic ego providing a wider view. Renaissance perspective might be called Ghiberti perspective because I find it first used by the 15th century Florentine artist Lorenzo Ghiberti. I find Renaissance perspective used by the 15th and 16th century Florentine and Venetian artists Masaccio, Botticelli, Leonard, Raphael, Michelangelo, Giovanni Bellini, Georgione and Titian.

Egyptian Perspective, found in the art of ancient North Africa and Egypt, is based on the whole composition being first seen nonaligned. Individual forms are the seen in this context reduced in scale and bottom aligned with a small visual.

Perspective Variations can help identify the origin of a work of art. These include a *wide view* which is the product of an ego larger than a composition. When the ego does not move relative to a composition I call it *fixed*. When the apparent distance between ego and object is increased I call it *reduced scaled*. Forms may be seen *side aligned, center aligned or bottom aligned. Disconnection* divides a compositions by following shapes first being seen nonaligned, on an entire composition being seen nonaligned. In this wide view context individual forms are seen bottom aligned with a small egos standing back from the composition.

Perspective and The History of Art

The following observations concern the use of the visual ego and its importance for art. They are not presented as authoritative. I leave it to the reader to use the perspectives described to decide if they are correct. In general I mention only works that do not depend the standard perspective of a region or a period unless a work has particular historical significance. I begin with the peoples of Sub Saharan Africa and African perspective. I find these peoples led the way in the peopling of the earth, domesticating plants and animals and the creation of civilization. Following this I go on to the Oceanic perceptive, European perspective, Oriental perspective, North African perspective, Semitic perspective and Indo European peripheral perspective.

The Early History of African Perspective
The prevailing theory is that Homo Sapiens Sapiens, modern human beings, originated in sub Saharan Africa 150,000 to 100,000 years ago. Archeology places them in the Levant around 90,000 B.C. and in Western Europe, Australia and perhaps China 40,000 years ago. Early works of art coming from a 'path' stretching from the sub-Saharan Africa, across the Middle East to India are based on African perspective, shapes are first seen blocked out by being nonaligned and then with a close by center aligned small ego so that shapes confront us in turn. Works of art coming from sub-Saharan Africa, the ancient Levant, the Mycenaean-Minoan civilization, the Ubaid period in northern Syria, Protoliterate Mesopotamia, 4th century B.C. Iran and the Indus Valley Civilization are based on African perspective.

Oceanic Perspective
Early works of art coming from South East Asia, Indonesia, Australia and Oceania are based on Oceanic perspective, shapes are first see nonaligned and then seen with a large center aligned visual ego that stands back from shapes. Both Oceanic and African perspective compositions are

based on first seen nonaligned shapes that confront as units. Oceanic perspective is a characteristic of works of art coming from South East Asia, Australia and Oceania.

Old Europe
The stone tools of Homo sapiens Neanderthalensis are nonaligned. See Neanderthal stone tools, 120,000-350,000 B.C., from Le Maustier, France, the British Museum. Flaked tools, ca. 70,000 B.C. from Howison's Port, South Africa, Pit Rivers Museum, Oxford, England are based on African perspective. This difference suggests that alignment is unique to Homo sapiens sapiens. Modern human beings are thought to have arrived in Western Europe 40,000 years ago. There are Upper Paleolithic works of art from Western Europe based on European perspective, shapes are first seem nonaligned like African perspective but then side aligned with a small ego that stands back from object. These include carvings in stone, ivory and bone and wall paintings from France and Spain. See *Venus of Willendorf*, ca. 30,000 B.C. Natural History Museum, Vienna. Neolithic works of art based on European perspective from the sixth through the fourth millennium B.C. include the ceramics of the Starcevo, Karanovo, Linearbandkermik, Bukk, Butmir, Vinca, Tisza and Lengyel cultures. The Cucuteni culture of Moldavia and the Western Ukraine is an exception among the Neolithic cultures of Central and Eastern Europe in it being based on nonaligned and the close by center aligned African perspective. African perspective is also used by the Thessalian Sesklo Culture. European perspective is a characteristic of Neolithic works of art from Spain, France, Switzerland, Ireland, Britain, Poland, Germany, Scandinavia, Italy and the western Mediterranean islands of Corsica, Sardinia, Sicily, Malta and Gozo.

Egyptian Art
Ancient Egyptian art for most of its history is based on North African perspective, and entire composition is first seen nonaligned and then individual elements seen bottom aligned with a small ego. This perspective is also used for works of art coming from Paleolithic North Africa, notably the Algerian Neolithic Tassili Culture, 7000-6000 B.C. *Giant Masked Figure.* cave painting, Tassili's n'Ager, Algeria. From the Baderian

Culture, 4000-3800 B.C. of the prehistoric Nile Valley come works of art based on African perspective. Works from the Nile valley Nagada Culture, 4000-2792, B.C. are based on North African perspective. See *Vase with Boat and Flamingoes*, 3500-3100 B.C. Egyptian Muscum, Cairo. This suggests a migration into the Nile Valley of peoples from North Africa, the future Egyptians, during the upper paleolithic. Early in the 4th millennium B.C. North and South Egypt are united, Egyptian art from this time until the second half of the second 8th century B.C., is based on North African perspective. See: *Narmer Pallet*, ca. 3000 BC, Egyptian Museum, Cairo; *Menkaure and His Queen*, ca. 2599 BC Museum of Fine Arts, Boston; the *Temple of Amon-Re Karnak*, begun ca. 1930 B.C.; the *Tomb of the Vizier Ramose*, ca. 1355 BC, west of Thebes; the *Treasures of Tutankamun*, ca. 1327 BC, Egyptian Museum, Cairo; the *Temples of Abu Simbel*, ca. 1250 BC and the *Golden Mask of Psusennes I*, 1039-991 BC Egyptian Museum, Cairo. Art from the reign of the Akhenaten, 1353-1337 BC, depends on wide view Oriental perspective. See *Stele of Akhenaten and Nefertiti with Their Three Daughters*, ca. 1345 BC, Egyptian Museum, Berlin. During the eighth and seventh century BC the art of the Kushite kingdom of southern Egypt produces Egyptian in style works based on African perspective. See *Statue of Montuemhet*, ca. 660 BC, Egyptian Museum, Cairo. Following the expulsion of the Nubians, the art of the 26th Dynasty, 664-525 BC is in the Egyptian style, but based on Semitic perspective, reduced scale forms in space. This perspective will persist through the Persian into the Macedonian occupations, around 144 BC when Hellenic perspective is introduced. See the Hellenic perspective *Temple at Efu*, 116 BC. The use of Hellenic perspective will persists into the first century AD. See the variously dates *Mummy Portraits* from the Faiyum, Cairo Museum.

The Ancient Near East
From the tenth, seventh and sixth millennium B.C. Neolithic Anatolia, Gobekli Tepe, 9600-8200 BC and Catal Huyuk, 7400-6200 BC, come works based on a version of Semitic perspective, the continuously aligned small center aligned small ego. See *Catal Huyuk Mother*, ca. 7000 BC, Museum of Anatolia Civilization, Ankara. Works from bronze age Mesopotamia are based on Semitic perspective which replaces African

perspective in Mesopotamia and Iran. The small static ego, forms not in space, is a characteristic of Summerian, Akkadian, Babylonian and Assyrian Art. See: *Standard of Ur,* 2600 BC, British Museuml *Stele of Hammurabi,* ca. 1760 BC, the Louvre and the *Istar Fate,* from Babylon, 525 BC, State Museum Berlin. Seventh century BC. Assyrian art from the reign of Ashurbanipal is based on side aligned Hellenic perspective, See *Dying Lioness,* 650 BC, British Museum.t

The Far East
Works of art coming from the Far East including China, Japan, South East Asia and Central and North East Asia are based on Oriental perspective. Oriental perspective depends on making our visual ego larger than an object. The Oriental perspective visual ego is placed back from the object. Oriental perspective objects are seen across space and spread out in front of us and they appear planar compared to Semitic perspective objects. Again succeeding objects are seen in a continuous space if aligned to the ego before we move. Chinese art is centrally aligned while art from elsewhere in the East is side aligned. See, Chinese *Bronze Ritual Vessels,* Chia Dynasty, 1523-1028 BC, Freer Gallery, Washington, DC and *Travelers on a Mountain Path,* Sung Dynasty, 960-1279 A.D. Taipei Palace Museum, Taiwan. An initial large ego wide view becomes a standard with Chinese art in the 14th century A.D. See *The Pavilion of Purple Fungus and a Rock Border,* Ni Tsan (1301-1374), Juan Dynasty, National Palace Museum, Taipei. Japanese art differs from Chinese art by forms being side aligned. See the Japanese *Dotako Bell,* 200 BC-200 AD, National Museum, Tokyo and the *Heigi Marogatami,* hand scroll, 1185-1333 A.D., Kamakura Period, the Museum of Fine Arts, Boston.

Pre-Columbian Art of the Americas
Side aligned Oriental perspective forms are characteristic of the Pre-Columbian art of North, Central and South America, the original inhabitants coming from Asia. See *Coatlicue,* 15th century A.D., National Anthropological Museum, Mexico City and *Portrait Jar (Mochica),* 400-100 A.D., Collection Norbert Mayrock, Santiago Chile. Today the art of the Native Americans of North America and that of the people of Central and South American continues to be is largely based on

Oriental perspective. See Oscary Niemeyer, *Palace of the Golden Dawn*, 1959, Brasilia, Brazil.

Indo European Art
The early art of peoples speaking the Indo-European family of languages is distinguished by use of peripheral perspective which places the small visual ego to the side of an object with forms seen peripherally aligned in sequence. This includes fourth millennium B.C. works from sites in the southern Ukraine, perhaps the Indo-European homeland; Hittite art; early Greek art; Celtic art; early German art; early Slavic art; early Baltic art; early Persian art, Indian art and Tocharian art. Mid second millennium B.C. peripheral perspective works of art coming from the mid Danube Valley indicate that by this time Indo-European speakers including the Greeks were in this area.

Mycenean-Minoan Art of the Aegean and the First Greek Art
Neolithic works of art of the Sesklo culture of the Thessalian plain in central Greece go back to the 7th millennium BC. These are based on African Perspective, shapes are first seen nonaligned and then center aligned with the small ego. See the *Sesklo Cup*, 5900-5800 B.C., Volos Museum, Greece. The same perspective is used by the Mycenean/Minoan civilization and Neolithic and Bronze Age works from the southern Greek mainland, various Aegean islands and Crete. See the *Lion Gate*, Mycenae, ca 1250 B.C. and the *Harvester Vase*, ca 1500 B.C., Heraklion Museum. Late Bronze Age works of art from Crete are based on a wide view Oriental perspective, See *Sarcophagus with Animals from Gournia*, no, 9499, ca 1200 B.C., Heraklion Museum. From Crete, the Southern Greek mainland and various islands come small second half of the second millennium B.C. works in clay that are based not on Mycenae/Minoan African perspective, but on center aligned peripheral perspective forms. It is a perspective used in Western Greece from the tenth to the late sixth century B.C. See *Dancing Clay Figurines*, ca 1200 B.C., Heraklion Museum. It would seem these relatively humble works were made by the Greek speaking people who we know from Linear B were part of the Mycenean/Minoan Civilization. Of interest here are mid second millennium B.C. works from the mid Danube valley,

based on peripheral perspective, that tells us the Greeks first came into Greece from this area. See *Wheeled Duck Vehicle*, ca 1500 B.C., Belgrade National Museum.

Greek Geometric Art
Eleventh and Tenth century B.C. painted pots from the Karimeikos cemetery in Athens are based on African perspective, a small ego center aligned to shapes first seen nonaligned. This is the perspective used for the *Dipylon Vase*, Dipylon Master, ca. 750 B.C. and *Dipylon Head*, ca 590 B.C. both National Museum, Athens. The *Kouros*, from Attica, ca 600 B.C. Metropolitan Museum of Art, N.Y.C. is base on small ego side aligned to shapes first seen nonaligned. These perspectives seem a survival of the Mycenean/Minoan period. Elsewhere in the Greek world, peripheral perspective is used until the last quarter of the sixth century B.C. In the west forms are seen center aligned. See *Kleobis and Biton*, 580 B.C. Delphi Museum, In the east forms are seen side aligned. See *Auxere Goddess*, ca 635 B.C. The Louvre.

Archaic Greek Art; Archermos, Phaidimos and Antenor.
An initial wide view distinguishes the sculpture of Archermos, Phaidimos and Antenor, the first two were active during the Archaic period, sixth century B.C., while the third, Antenor is from the Early Classical period. To Archermos of Chios, is attributed the *Nike from Delos*, Athens National Museum, inscribed on the base and *Kore no.675*, Acropolis Museum, also inscribed. Both from the mid sixth century B.C. and based on view side aligned peripheral perspective. From slightly later come two works by the Athenian sculptor Phaidimos, *The Calf Bearer*, Acropolis Museum, inscribed and the *Peplos Kore*, Acropolis Museum, attributed by me on the basis of style and the use of a wide-view small ego center aligned peripheral perspective. The works of Antenor of Athens, based on wide-view small ego center aligned Semitic perspective date from the late sixth into the early fifth century B.C. These include: *Kore 681*, inscribed; *Kore 671*, on the basis of style and perspective, both in the Acropolis Museum, Athens, the *Thesus and Antiope* from the *Temple of Apollo*, Eretria, Chalkida Museum, on the bais of style and perspective; the surviving *Sculpture of the East pediment of the Temple*

of Apollo, Delphi, on the basis of perspective; the *Metopes, Treasury of the Athenians*, Delphi Museum, on the basis of perspective and most importantly, the *Head and Torso of Aristogeiton*, ca. 475, Conservatory Museum, Rome, which I find to be an original on the basis of style and perspective. The *Aristogeiton* is from Antenor's famous *Tyranacides Group* that once stood in the Athenian Agora.

Phidias.
The great Athenian sculptor Phidias follows Antenor in leading the way to the Classical style. Phidias use of the fixed ego is unique in Antiquity until Lysippos in the fourth century B.C. On the basis of style and the fixed ego I identify Phidias as the Olympia Master, the creator of the *Pedimental Sculptures of the Temple of Zeus*, Olympia, 471-456 BC, Olympia Museum, which are based on center aligned fixed-ego Semitic perspective. The coherence provide by the fixed ego which is use to balance of large and small three-dimensional units and the blend of naturalism and abstraction dramatically presents the subjects depicted in the pediments The *Temple of Zeus Metopes*, Olympia Museum, are based on Semitic perspective center aligned forms and lack the precision and coherence of the Phidias' pediments. The same difference exists between *Zeus from Artemisium*, ca.455 B.C., Athens National Museum, which I attribute to Phidias on the basis of style and the fixed ego and its contemporary the *Charioteer*, ca 460 B.C. Delphi Museum which is based on center aligned Semitic perspective forms, The *Charioteer* is relatively static. Forms are experienced in sequence rather than as a moment in time. Both the *Ludouvisi "Throne,"* ca. 460 B.C. Altemps Museum, Rome and the *Boston "Throne,"* ca, 447, Museum of Fine Arts, Boston, are based on the center aligned fixed ego and so I believe by Phidias. The difference in style between these two is explained by a difference in date and perspective. The *Ludouvisi "Throne,"* ca. 460 B.C. is based on center aligned fixed-ego. Semitic perspective. The *Boston "Throne,"* ca. 447 B.C. is based on center aligned fixed-ego Attic perspective, the ego as a point aligned with a point beyond the object. The *Boston "Throne"* represents a new stage in Phidias' career. Fixed-ego Attic perspective more precisely defines three-dimensional form and dramatically enriches the large scale relationship between figures as seen on the front of the *Boston*

"Throne." The I also see the *Parthenon* as a Phidias design. It is based on frontal aligned fixed ego Attic perspective which gives it its clearly hierarchy of form and great three dimensional coherence. On the basis of their being based on center aligned fixed-ego Attic perspective forms I identify two of the *Metopes* from the *Parthenon Outer South Frieze, 1* and 30, British Museum as by Phidias. I also identify the now wide view center aligned fixed ego Attic perspective slab, *Inner Frieze, West VIII*, Athens, Acropolis Museum as by Phidias. This is the perspective used in the final stage of Phidias' career. All other *Parthenon Metopes* are based on center aligned Attic perspective. The inner frieze is based on center aligned wide-view Attic perspective. The *Parthenon Pediment Sculptures,* ca 435 B.C. now mostly in the British Museum with a few in Athens are based on Phidias' wide-view center aligned fixed-ego Attic perspective. The difference between Phidias' final two perspectives is also demonstrated by the *Riace Warriors,* Reggio Museum, Italy, which I attribute to Phidias on the basic of fixed ego center aligned Attic perspective. *Warrior A* is based on center aligned fixed-ego Attic perspective. *Warrior B* is based on wide-view center aligned fixed-ego Attic perspective. The difference in perspective accounts for the leap in coherence between *A* and *B*. the fluidity and simultaneity of *Warrior B* makes it one of the a supreme achievements of the Classical Period.

These works dating from ca 470 B.C. to ca 430 B.C. on the basis of documentation, style and the use of three different fixed-ego perspectives I find to be originals by Phidias: The *Ludouvisi "Throne,"* Altemps Museum, Rome, ca. 460 BC, fixed-ego center aligned Semitic perspective.

1. The *Pediment Sculptures Temple of Zeus,* Olympia, Olympia Museum, 471-456 B.C. fixed-ego center aligned Semitic perspective.
2. The *Zeus from Artemision,* National Museum, Athens, ca. 455 B.C. fixed-ego center aligned Semitic perspective.
3. Head *of Apollo,* Kassel Type, Conservatore Museum, ca. 455 BC, fixed-ego center aligned Semitic perspective.
4. *Warrior A,* from Riace, Reggio Calabria Museum, ca. 450 BC, fixed-ego center aligned Attic perspective.

5. *Boston "Throne,"* Museum of Fine Arts, Boston, ca. 447 BC, fixed center aligned Attic perspective.

6. *The Parthenon*, the Acropolis, Athens, begun 447 BC, fixed-ego center aligned Attic perspective.

7. *Parthenon Metopes, S1 and S30*, British Museum, ca. 445 BC, fixed-ego center aligned Attic perspective.

8. *Parthenon Frieze, Slab VII, West Frieze*, 440-432 BC, Acropolis Museum, wide view center aligned fixed ego Attic perspective.

9. *Parthenon Pediment Sculptures*, British Museum and Acropolis Museum, ca. 435 BC, wide-view center aligned fixed-ego Attic perspective.

10. *Athena Parthenos Statuette and Shield*, Patras Museum, ca. 435 BC wide-view center aligned fixed-ego Attic perspective.

11. *"Omphalos Apollo,"* Athens National Museum, ca. 435 BC, wide-view fixed-ego center aligned Attic perspective.

12. *Warrior B*, from Riace, Reggio Calabria Museum, ca. 435 BC, wide-view fixed-ego center aligned Attic perspective.

13. and 15. *Two Torsos in Greek Dress*, Metropolitan Museum of Art, ca. 450 B.C. wide-view center aligned fixed-ego Attic perspective.

Fifth Century Classical Greek Art.

The most influential style in history of art is that coming from fifth and fourth century Greece, Greek Classical Art. Toward the beginning of the last quarter of the sixth century B.C. Greek artists changed from using peripheral perspective to Semitic perspective which related in more coherent more three dimensional forms. In the middle of the fifth century as seen in the work of Phidias Athenian artists adopt Attic perspective which results in a more precise definition of three-dimensional form. Elsewhere in Greece the norm is center aligned Semitic perspective forms in the West and center aligned Semitic perspective forms in the East. The Greek Classical composition is balanced, three-dimensional and harmonious. The Classical figure harmoniously combines the natural and geometric abstract. For most of the Classical period the young, idealized, nude male figure is the principal subject. The Classical Style contrasts with the more rigid Hard or Early Classical Style of the first half of the fifth century. (The so called *Kritian Boy*, Acropolis Museum, is not a milestone in the development of the Classical style. The body is based on Attic perspective and would date ca. 450 B.C. The head which I see as not belonging to the body is based on side view Hellenic perspective and in my opinion modern Greek). Original works in the Classical style include the *Propylaea*, 437-432 B.C. and *Erectheun*, Acropolis Athens, including the *Frieze* and *Porch of the Maidens, 421-400* B.C. The original *Maidens* and *Frieze* are now in the Acropolis Museum. Both are based on center aligned Attic Perspective as is the *Hephesteion* including the *Frieze*, begun 449 BC, Athenian Agora. I find a number of Athenian Grave Stele from the second half of the fifth century to be based on center aligned Attic perspective including the *Cat Stele*, ca 430 B.C. and the *Stele of Hegeso*, ca. 400 B.C. both in the Athens National Museum. Not long after the mid century, led perhaps by the Achilles Painter, vase painting comes to be based on center aligned Attic perspective. See Achilles Amphora, ca 440 B.C., Vatican Museums. Also based on center aligned Attic perspective is the Alcamenes' original the *Prokne and Itys*, ca 435 B.C., Acropolis Museum. Kresalis, a follower of Phidias from Crete I find to be responsible for several center aligned Attic perspective works including the *Portrait of Pericles*, ca. 425 B.C., the British Museum, the *Head and Shoulders of Athena*, ca. 415 BC, the Glyptotek, Munich (The *Athena Velletri* in the Louvre is a Roman copy of the entire statue) and the *Head of Diomedes*, ca 435 B.C., the Museum of Fine Arts, Boston. Wide-view center aligned fixed ego Attic perspective as seen in the later work of Pheidias is not widely used. I it is used for the *Temple of Athena Nike*, the Acropolis, including the *Balustrade Nike Frieze*, ca 420 B.C., Acropolis Museum, Athens. Classical style works from outside Attica are based on Semitic perspective forms in space in the West and no space in the East.

Fourth Century Late Classical Art,
There are no major perspective changes in Classical Attic works of art from the first half of the fourth century B.C. Semitic perspective center alignment is the norm beyond Athens. See the *Temple of Apollo*, Bassae, the Pelloponneses, ca. 400 B.C. The *Esklepion*, Epidauros, 380-70 B.C. and *Temple of Athena Alea*, Tegea, ca. 340 B.C. In Athens Attic perspective is the standard. Kephisodothos status, *Peace Holding the Infant Wealth*, ca. 370 B.C. once stood in Athens. I find that the headless body, minus Pluto in the Metropolitan Museum of Art, New York City, to be based on center aligned Attic perspective, forms in space and so an original. I find that the head of *Peace* based on a Greco-Roman body at one time on loan from Italy to the Museum of Fine Arts, Boston, to be based on the same Attic perspective and so the original head. The *Stele of Dexilios*, ca. 390 B.C., Kerameikos Museum and the *Villa Albani Stele*, ca. 390 B.C. Rome, are both based on center aligned Attic perspective. The so-called *Mausoleum*, Halicarnassus, 359-351 BC, the British Museum are based on center aligned Attic perspective, as is the *Column Drum* from the *Temple of Artemis*, Ephesus, ca. 320, British Museum. The *Demeter from Cnidos*, c. 325 BC, the British Museum and the *Marathon Boy*, ca 320, National Museum, Athens.

Praxiteles.
The principal subject of Classical Greek art is the idealized, young, male nude. In the mid fourth century the Athenian sculptor Praxiteles, the son of Kephisodothos makes the first life sized status of an idealized, young female nude, the famous *Cinidian Aphrodite*, ca 350 B.C., that is now lost. There is, however, in the Heraklion Museum a wide view center aligned Attic perspective half sized headless *Torso of the Cinidian* from Gortyna, Crete. This on the basis of style and the use of wide-view center aligned Attic perspective I find it to be an original by Praxiteles. In the same Heraklion Museum Gallery is a *Head of Aphrodite* also based on wide-view center aligned Attic perspective, at present on a Greco-Roman garden statue form Gortyna. It appears this head belongs on the torso. On the basis of the use of wide view center aligned Attic perspective that I find to be unique to Praxiteles I believe the following to be originals by Praxiteles: *Pan*, ca. 350 B.C., in the Heraklion Museum;

a crouching *Aphrodite*, ca. 350 BC, Altemps Museum, Rome and most marvelous of all, a clothed *Aphrodite*, ca. 350 B.C., Rethymnon Museum, Crete. Its sate of preservation is amazing, her skin retains its polish, the transparent drapery around her torso is wonderfully rendered and the drapery that flows her hips is like rushing water. She sets the standard against which all surviving Classical works of art should be measured. She may well be the clothed *Kos Aphrodite* mentioned by Pliny. The face is visualized to a degree that perhaps makes It may depict Praxiteles famous mistress, Phyrne.

Lysippos
Lysippos of Sycon, active ca. 365-339 BC, is the master sculptor of the second half of the 4th century B.C. It may be that it was Lysippos who introduced Hellenic perspective to the Greek world. I find the use of a fixed-ego side aligned Hellenic perspective to be unique to Lysippos in Antiquity. No originals by the prolific Lysippos are believed to have survived. However, I find on the basis of style and fixed-ego side aligned Hellenic perspective that the famous *Apoxyomenos*, ca. 350 BC, Vatican Museums, attributed to Lysippos by Pliny, is the original. Also on the basis of style and fixed ego side aligned Hellenic perspective I find the following to be originals by Lysippos: The *Lembach Hercules*, ca 345 B.C., Altemps Museum, Rome; the *Antikythera Youth*, ca 335 B.C., Athens National Museum; the *Erbach Head of Alexander*, ca 335 B.C., Acropolis Museum and the famous *Hermes and the Infant Dionysos*, ca 330 B.C., Olympia Museum. The *Apoxymenos* is closest to high Classical in style although Lysippos' Hellenic perspective forms are less precise. The *Antikythera Youth* is a further step from the fifth century, while the *Olympia Hermes* in the flow of its forms and soft yet deep modeling are again something new.

Other Athenian works on the basis of style and Attic perspective, forms in space, from the latter half of the fourth century that I find originals are: the *Head of Dionysos*, ca. 330 BC, from the *Temple of Apollo*, Delphi, Delphi Museum; the *Euboleus*, ca. 340 BC, from the Eleusis and the *Stele from the Ilissos*, ca. 330 BC, Athens National Museum.

The Hellenistic Period.
The Hellenistic period is the Greek world from the death of Alexander the Great, 323 BC, to the battle of Actium, 31 BC. Hellenic perspective, forms not in space is variously used. Semitic center aligned perspective is standard for Western Greek art including the Greek cities of Italy and Sicily. Semitic perspective, forms not in space is the norm in the East including the Macedonia and Seleucid kingdoms. Hellenic perspective is prevalent in Athens during the last quarter of the 4th century BC and during the Hellenistic period. Examples include *Agias*, ca. 330 BC, Delphi Museum; the *Stele of Demetria and Pamphile*, ca. 320 BC, Kermeikos Museum; the *Stele of Aristonautes*, ca. 320 B.C. Athens National Museum and the *Themis*, ca. 300 BC, from Rhammous, by Chairestratos, Athens National Museum. On the basis of coins I find that Hellenic perspective migrated from Athens to Pergamon in the first quarter of the 3rd century BC where it is responsible for the *Great Altar of Zeus*, 190 BC, Pergamon Museum, Berlin. The *Altar* is a work characterized by heightened emotion and a shift from the Classical balance between the large and the small elements that favors the large. The *Aphrodite form Melos*, second century BC, the Louvre, is based on side aligned Hellenic perspective. The Hellenic perspective works connected with Rhodes based on side aligned Hellenic perspective are the *Winged Victory of Samothrace*, ca 190 B.C. the Louvre; the *Head of Helios*, 3rd century B.C., Rhodes Museum and the *Laocoon*, ca 200 B.C., the Vatican Museums. Delos with its ties to Athens is another place where Hellenic perspective was used. From Delos comes the side aligned Hellenic perspective, *Aphrodite, Eros and Pan*, late second century B.C. and the *Bronze Portrait Head*, ca. 200 BC, both in the Athens National Museum. Around 144 BC Egyptian art comes to be based on Hellenic perspective which persists there into the 1st century AD. See variously dated *Faiyum Portraits*. Cairo Museum.

Villa Novan, Etruscan and Roman Republican Art
Bronze age works of art, ceramic pots and metal implements, from the north Italian Villa Nova Culture, 8th century B.C., Tarquinia Museum, Italy, are based on European perspective, shapes first seen nonaligned and then side aligned with a small ego. The Villa Novan culture would

seem to be a survival of Old Europe. Etruscan perspective is based on first seen nonaligned then to side aligned the peripheral perspective ego. See *Apollo from Veii*, ca 510 B.C., Villa Giullia Museum, Rome. Etruscan perspective survives into the 1st century BC in Etruria and Rome. In the Greek Southern Italy and Sicily center aligned Semitic perspective is standard. In the mid first century B.C. Etruscan perspective is replaced in Rome by nonalignment followed by center aligned Semitic perspective. In the Greek east the perspective becomes side aligned Semitic perspective after nonalignment This change would seem to stem from the Island of Delos. During the second century BC Delos is a center for the slave trade and a point of contact between Rome and Athens. This perspective is found in Roman art of the next two and a half centuries. The *Augustus from Prima Porta*, ca. 20 AD. Vatican Museums, exemplifies the Western version.

Art of the Roman Empire, First Through the ThirdCenturies AD
With Semitic perspective comes a new style in Rome, the Julio Claudian, a revival of the Greek Classicism using center aligned semitic perspective after nonalignment. This isolates parts providing for their individuality in contrast to the homogeneity of the Greek Classical style. Compare the statue of *Augustus from Prima* and its source, the two *Statues in Greek Dress* that I attribute to Phidias, ca. 440 BC, Metropolitan Museum of Art, New York City. Early in the third century BC Roman art in the West, perhaps beginning in North Africa, turns to side aligned peripheral perspective. See the *Arch of Septimius Severus*, Rome, 203 A.D. and the *Arch of Septimius Severus* Leptis Magna, ca. 205 A.D. both based on side aligned peripheral perspective. Peripheral perspective results in compositions made up of multiple separate parts. This compartmentalizing of works grows stronger as the century progresses. See the *Constantinian Reliefs* on the *Arch of Constantine* and the composition of the *Arch* as a whole, 312-315 A.D. Rome.

Early Christian and Byzantine Art.
Fourth century A.D. early Christian art from Italy is based on side aligned peripheral perspective. See the *Sarcophagus of Junius Bassus*, ca. 359 A.D., St. Peter's Rome, and the *Mosaics of St. Vitale*, ca. 547 AD,

Ravenna, Italy. The *Balustrade of the Patriarch Sigvald*, ca. 715- 750 A.D. Cathedral Baptistry, Cividale, Italy is based on side aligned peripheral perspective. As the Greek speaking Eastern Roman Empire becomes the Byzantine Empire, center aligned peripheral perspective is standard. See great Justinian church, *Hagia Sophia*, 532-535 AD, Istanbul. Following the iconoclastic period, eighth and ninth century AD, center aligned Hellenic perspective, becomes standard in the Greek speaking world as it is today. See the 14th century fresco, *Harrowing of Hell*, 1310-20 AD, *Church of Christ in Chora*, Istanbul.

Islamic Art
In sixth and seventh centuries A.D. a new religion and culture, that of Islam, swept the Near East and Southern Mediterranean world. Within twenty years Arabia, Syria, Egypt, Iraq and Iran are converted followed by the development of an Islamic art. In the East, including Egypt, the standard perspective is side aligned Semitic perspective. See *Dome of the Rock*, 690 A.D. the Temple Mount, Jerusalem. In the West, North Africa and Spain, the standard is bottom aligned reduced scale Semitic perspective perhaps a partial survival from prehistoric North Africa, See *The Great Mosque*, 985 AD, Cordova, Spain. The Islamic art of the Turkish Ottoman Empire is based on continuous side aligned Semitic perspective forms. See the Mosque of Ahmed I, 1109-16, Istanbul.

Early Medieval Art, Western Europe
Europe from the mid second millennium B.C. into the sixth century A.D. is entered by the Indo-European speaking peoples Celts, Germans, Slaves and Balts. The early art of these peoples is based on side aligned peripheral perspective. See: *Sutton Hoo Treasure*, Saxon, seventh century AD, the British Museum, London; the *Book of Kells*, ca. 800 A.D. Trinity College Library, Dublin; the Carolingian, *Utrecht Psalter*, 820-832 AD, University Library, Utrecht, the Netherlands. See *Abbey Church of St. Michael*, 1001-1033, Hildesheim Germany. Early Romanesque is a name given to Western European art ca 1050 to 1200 when the Gothic style begins to replace the Romanesque. Romanesque art is largely based on side aligned peripheral perspective. The change to frontal perspective

I find begins in Catalonia in the eleventh century and moves north in stages.

Art from Medieval Spain
In the early eighth century A.D. except for the Christian Visogothic Kingdoms to the north, Asturias-Leon, Navarre and Aragon al of Spain including Catalonia become Islamic. The art of the Visogothic Kingdoms into the 12th century is based on Indo European side aligned peripheral perspective. See the *Portals of San Isidro* ca. 1110 AD, Leon. In contrast, the Islamic art of the south, al Andulas, is based on reduced scale bottom aligned Semitic perspective. See the *Great Mosque*, eighth to tenth century AD, Cordova. In the eleventh century the Caliphate of Cordova breaks into smaller "kingdoms" while the Christian kingdoms strengthen. At this time reduced scale bottom aligned Semitic perspective replaces peripheral perspective in Catalonia. See *Lintel, Saint-Gens-des-Fontains*, 1020, French Catalonia. This new perspective will become the standard for Spain and continues to be so today.

Art from Medieval France.
During the twelfth century there is a transition in France from center aligned peripheral perspective to center aligned Semitic perspective, which becomes the standard for French art from this time on. The progress to frontal perspective begins in the south. See *St. Sernin*, 1070-1120, Toulouse; *Notre-Dame-la*-Grande, early 12th century, Poitiers and *St. Gilles du Garde*, mid 12th century, all based on center aligned frontal perspective, forms in space. The architecture and decoration of the famous Romanesque churches to the north including *Saint Pierre*, 1115-1130, Moissac; the *Cathedral of Notre-Dame*, 1145-1150, Chartes. The *Cathedral of Notre Dame*, 1163-1250, Paris, is based on center aligned Semitic perspective as is the French Gothic art that follows.

Medieval Art from England and Germany
In England as in Spain and France there is a progress from peripheral perspective to Semitic perspective. *Salisbury Cathedral*, begun 1220, is based on center aligned peripheral perspective while the *Crossing Tower*, 1334, is based on side aligned Semitic perspective the new standard

English perspective. In Germany Semitic perspective, forms not in space replaces peripheral perspective in the 16th century and becomes the standard. See the side aligned peripheral perspective *Freiberg Cathedral*, 1260-1350, Germany. There is a cultural lag in respect to the change to Semitic perspective in Europe, South to North and West to East.

Medieval Art form Sicily and Italy
Semitic arrived in Italy by way of Sicily where Norman replaces Moorish rule at the end of the eleventh century, 1091. Rather than use Norman, continuous center aligned peripheral perspective, the Norman Christians probably used Moorish artists who used reduced scaled bottom aligned Semitic-perspective, a variation on the Semitic perspective used in North Africa. See *Mosaics of Monreal Cathedral*, 1180-90, Sicily. Semitic perspective it would seem migrated to Italy from Sicily, moving south to north during the thirteenth century, see *Castel del Monte*, hunting lodge of the Emperor, Frederick II, ca 1240 Apulia, Italy, reduced scaled center aligned Semitic perspective. In contrast *Santa Croce*, Florence, begun 1295, and the *Doge's Palace*, Venice, begun 1304 are based on center aligned peripheral perspective. The Florentine Giotto di Bondone leads the transition to frontal perspective. Giotto's uses wide-view center aligned reduced scale Semitic perspective. See transition to frontal perspective. Giotto's uses wide-view center aligned reduced scale Semitic perspective. See Giotto's powerfully coherent frescos in the *Scrovengi Chapel Frescos*, 1305, Padua. I find the brothers Lorenzetti introducing frontal perspective to Siena. See Ambrogio's reduced scaled continuous center aligned *Allegories of Good and Bad Government*, 1338-40, Palazzo Publico, Siena and Pietro's reduced scale center aligned Semitic perspective *Birth of the Virgin*, 1335-42, Museo dell Opera de Duomo, Siena. The change from peripheral perspective to Semitic perspective is documented by the difference between Nicolo Pisano's center aligned peripheral perspective *Pulpit*, 1259-60, the Baptistry, Pisa and Giovanni Pisano's reduced scale center aligned Semitic perspective *Pulpit*, 1302-10, Pisa Cathedral. In the early 14th century reduced scale center aligned Semitic perspective begins becoming the Italian standard.

Renaissance Perspective and the Early Renaissance in Florence and Italy
I find that Renaissance perspective first appearing the in a work of Lorenzo Ghiberti the illegitimate, twenty year old adopted son of a goldsmith and the winner of a competition to design the *North Doors of the Baptistry of S. Giovanni*, 1402, Florence. See Ghiberti's winning wide view fixed ego reduced scale center aligned fixed ego Renaissance persecutive *Competition Piece, The Sacrifice of Isaac*, 1401-2, Bargello Museum, Florence. Ghiberti's perspective is unique at the time for its combination of Renaissance perspective a wide-view and a fixed-ego. Compare Ghiberti's competition piece to Filippo Brunelleschi's *Competition Piece, Sacrifice of Isaac* also in the Bargello. The Brunelleschi which is based on disconnected reduced scale center aligned Semitic perspective is composed of individual passages. Ghiberti's piece in contrast presents us with a cataclysmic moment in time conveyed by the simultaneous actions of Abraham, Isaac and the Angel supported by everything else in the composition. Ghiberti's Works to follow include: *Designs for Stained Glass Windows*, the *Cathedral of Florence*, 1409; the *North Doors of Baptistry*, Florence, installed 1424; the statues of *St. John the Baptist* together with the *Niche*, 1417 and *St. Stephen*, 1424, both formally on *Or San Michele*, the *Casa di Zenobia*, 1442, Florence Cathedral; the incredible *East Doors* of the Baptistry, installed 1452, where jambs, frames, and panels are all seen from the same point of view. The *East Doors* presently on the *Baptistry* are inadequate copies based on standard Italian frontal perspective. Panels from the originals doors are on display in the Opera del Duomo Museum. *The Dome of the Cathedral of Florence*, completed 1436, long attributed to Filippo Brunelleschi the builder, is based on wide view center aligned fixed-ego Renaissance perspective, reduced scale forms as is the *Model for the Dome*, ca. 1418, Opera del Duomo Museum. Thus I find Lorenzo Ghiberti not Brunelleschi to be the designer of the *Dome of Florence Cathedral*. The works of Brunelleschi before ca 1420 are based on Semitic perspective, reduced scaled disconnected forms in space as is his *Competition Piece* and the *Opsidale deli Innocenti*, 1419, Florence. In about 1425 Brunelleschi invents linear perspective, a geometric procedure based on a fixed vanishing point that does not depend on a particular use of the visual ego. At about this time Brunelleschi's forms are seen in continuously

aligned. Brunelleschi's invention of linear perspective may have been inspired by the coherence of Ghiberti's work. Despite linear perspective Brunelleschi never discoveries the secret of Renaissance perspective. It seems also to be unknown to the architect, Leon Battista S Alberti, who wrote a treatise on painting that explains linear perspective. Alberti uses Attic perspective, reduced scale center aligned forms. See his *Palazzo Rucellai*, 1446-51, Florence. Ghiberti's influence is far reaching and of particularly importance for artists who worked with him. These include Michelozzo di Bartolomeo who's *St. Matthew*, 1422, for Or San Michele, usually attributed to Ghiberti, is based on the wide-view reduced scale center aligned Semitic perspective, the perspective Michelozzo uses for the *Medici-Riccardi Palace*, 1444, Florence. Another who seems to have benefited from his Ghiberti connection is the sculptor Donatello. See his reduced scaled center aligned Attic perspective, *St. George*, 1415-17, for Or San Michele, Bargello Museum. The relief *St. George and the Dragon*, below the sculpture, is based on wide-view reduced scale center aligned Semitic perspective and is probably by Michelozzo. Donatello's *Jeremiah*, 1423-25 for the Campanile of the Cathedral, now in the Opera del Duomo Museum is based on wide-view center aligned reduced scale Attic perspective which will continue as Donatello's perspective. Another artist who may have benefitted from working with Ghiberti is Paolo Ucello. Ucello uses reduced scale center aligned fixed ego Renaissance perspective. See his *Sir John Hawkwood*, 1436, fresco, Florence Cathedral. The painter Benozzo Gossoli who worked with Ghiberti uses reduced scale center aligned wide view Semitic perspective, see his *Magi Frescos, Medici Palace*, 1459, Florence. His master Fra Angelico uses reduced scale center aligned Renaissance perspective. See his fresco *The Annunciation*, 1440-50, San Marco, Florence, The painter Massolino may have worked with Ghiberti. He uses reduced scale center aligned fixed-ego Semitic perspective. Massolino's young collaborator, Masaccio, used reduced scale center aligned fixed ego Renaissance perspective. See the *Frescos of the Brancacci Chapel*, 1425, Sta. Maria de Carmine, Florence where both Massolino and Masaccio employed Brunelleschi's new linear perspective. Fra Filippo Lippi who witnesses Massolino and Masaccio at work in the Brancacci Chapel, uses reduced scale center aligned Renaissance perspective. See *Madonna and Child*,

1437, National Gallery, Rome. Other fifteenth century Florentine artists using Renaissance perspective include the sculptor Bernardo Rossolino who uses reduced scale center aligned Renaissance perspective. See his *Tomb of Leonardo Bruni*, 1445, *Sta. Croce*, Florence. The architect Guilio da Maiano uses reduced scale center aligned fixed ego Renaissance perspective for the *Pazzi Chapel Porch*, 1461, Sta. Croce Florence. The sculptor Luca della Robbia also uses reduced scale center aligned Renaissance perspective. See his *Cantoria*, 1435, Opera del Duomo Museum. Andrea del Verrocchio, Leonardo's master uses reduced scale center aligned fixed-ego Renaissance perspective. See the *Equestrian Monument of Colleoni*, 1481-96, Venice. The same perspective is used by Sandro Botticelli. See *Primavera*, 1482 and *Birth of Venus*, 1484-6, Uffize Gallery, Florence. Another Florentine using reduced scale center aligned fixed ego Renaissance perspective is Domenico Ghirlandaio. See *Calling of St. Peter*, 1481, Sistine Chapel, the Vatican. The painter and sculptor Antonio Pollaiuolo uses this same perspective for the *Tomb of Sixtus IV*, 1489-93, St. Peter's, the Vatican. The Florentine painter Andrea del Castagno reduced scale continuously center aligned Semitic perspective. See *Last Supper*, 14450-50. S. *Apollonia*, Florence. Piero della Francesca, from the Tuscan town of Borgo San Sepolcro uses reduced scale center aligned fixed ego Renaissance perspective. See his frescos depicting *The Legend of the True Cross*, 1454-58, S. Francesco, Arezzo. Piero works in Florence as an assistant to Domenico Veneziano, who uses reduced scale center aligned Semitic perspective disconnected forms. See *St. Lucy Altarpiece*, 1445-47, Uffizi Gallery, Florence.

Fifteenth Century Venice and Italy
I find that Renaissance perspective was not used in Italy beyond Florence and Venice during fifteenth century. The leader of the Perugian school, the master of Raphael, Perugino, uses reduced scale continuously center aligned Semitic perspective together with linear perspective for *Christ Giving the Keys to St. Peter*, 1481, Sistine Chapel, the Vatican. Andrea Mantegna, originally near Padua and a brother-in-law of the Venice Bellinis, uses reduced scale center aligned fixed ego Semitic perspective facilitating his proto Mannerist geometric intricacy. See his *Altarpiece*, 1456-59, *San Zeno*, Verona. The fifteenth century Venetian

painter Giovanni Bellini uses reduced scale center aligned fixed ego Renaissance perspective. See the *Frari Altarpiece*, 1488, *Sta. Maria del Glorioso dei Frari*, Venice. Two other fifteenth century Venetian painters using reduced scale center aligned fixed ego Renaissance perspective are Carlo Crivelli and Antonio Vivarini. See Crivelli's *Madonna and Child*, 1477, Vatican Museums and Vivarini's *Saint Ambrose Polyptych*, 1482, Accademia, Venice. The Venitian Vittore Carpaccio uses reduced scale center aligned fixed-ego Semitic perspective. See *Dream of St. Ursula*, 1495, Accademia, Venice.

Early Renaissance in the North
French fifteenth century art is based on standard French perspective, center aligned Semitic perspective. See Claus Sluter's *Well of Moses*, 1395-1406, Chartreuse de Champ mol, Dijon, France. The *Avignon Pieta*, ca. 1445, the Louvre, considered by some to be French being based on reduced scale bottom aligned Semitic perspective and probably Spanish. Standard English perspective is side aligned Semitic perspective. See *Wilton Diptych*, ca. 1400, National Gallery of Art, London. Oil painting appears in the Souther Netherlands in the fifteenth century. See Robert Campin's *Merode Triptych*, 1425-32, Metropolitan Museum of Art, New York which is based on center aligned Semitic perspective. The left hand panel donor portraits are based on wide view center aligned Renaissance perspective suggesting the panel is by Rogier va der Wyden. Jan van Eyk, creates extraordinary paintings in oil based on wide view center aligned Hellenic perspective. See the Brothers van Eyk, *Ghent Altarpiece*, 1432, St. Bavo, Ghent. The use of Renaissance perspective first comes North in the work of Petrus Christus. See his center aligned fixed ego Renaissance perspective *Freidsam Annunciation*, ca. 1435, the Metropolitan Museum of Art, New York City. Rogier van der Wyden starts off using center aligned Semitic perspective, see *Decent from the Cross*, 1435, Prado Museum, Madrid. Later he turns to wide view center aligned fixed ego Renaissance perspective. See *Saint Luke Painting the Virgin*, 1435-40, the Museum of Fine Arts, Boston. Dirk Bouts, Hugo van der Goes and Hans Memling use wide view fixed ego center aligned Semitic perspective. See Bouts' *Last Supper*, 1464-68, St. Peter's Louvin, van der Goes' *Portinari Altarpiece*, ca. 1476, Uffizi Gallery, Florence and

Memling's *St. John Altarpiece*, ca. 1470, St, John's Hospital, Bruges. From the end of the 15th century and the beginning of the 16th comes the works of Hieronymous Bosch. He uses a wide view that includes the side panels fixed-ego center aligned Hellenic perspective for *Garden of Earthly Delights Triptych*, 14880-1515, the Prado Museum, Madrid.

India.
The art of the Indus Valley civilization, ca. 2500-1500 B.C. is based on African perspective. See *Storage Jar from Chandu-daro*, ca. 2000 BC, The Museum of Fine Arts, Boston. The early presumably lost art of the Indo-European speaking people who entered India ca. 1500 BC was probably based on side aligned peripheral perspective, which is the standard for Indian art to this day. See the *Great Stupa*, 3rd to the last 1st century B.C., Sanci; the art of the Kushan period including Gandharan Art from northwest India, 50-320 AD; the medieval Hindu *Frescos from the Ajanta Caves*, 500-550 A.D.; the art of the Pablava period, 500-750 A.D.; the *Temples of Orissa*, 8th to 13th century and the 11th century *Chola Bronzes*. The use of perspective continues during the Mughol dynasty, 1526- 1756. See the *Taj Mahal*, ca 16340-48, Agra, India.

The Far East and Southeast Asia
From its beginnings Chinese art is based on center aligned Oriental perspective. In the fourteenth century A.D., during the Juan Dynasty, 1280-1368, a period of Mongol domination, a wide-view center aligned Oriental perspective becomes the Chinese standard. See Ni Tsan's *Landscape*, ca. 1360, Freer Gallery, Washington, DC. This perspective will hold sway in China for the next four and half centuries producing an extended period of outstanding quality. Today in the late twentieth and early twenty-first century the wide view is being dropped by perhaps an effort to escape the past. Ironically a return to a narrower Oriental perspective is retreat to even more traditional Chinese Art.

Standard Japanese perspective is side aligned Oriental perspective. See the *The Heiji Monogotari*, a 12th century hand scroll, Museum of Fine Arts, Boston. The Zen master Hakuin Ekaku uses center aligned Oriental perspective, see The *Sound of One Hand*, 18th century, Private Collection. Another exception is Hiroshige Utagawa, who uses wide-view fixed-ego side aligned Semitic perspective. See his wood block print *Rain Shower over the Ohashi Bridge*, ca. 1840.

Buddhism and Hinduism have a far reaching influencer in Asia. In Nepal, Sri Lanka and for a time, Indonesia they appear to have carried with them side aligned peripheral perspective. See the *Frescos of the Great Rodi of Sigiruga*, 479-497 A.D. Sri Lanka and the *Temples of Borobudour*, late 8th century A.D. Java. Elsewhere in Southeast Asia and in the Far East; Tibet, Myanmar, Thailand, Cambodia, Vietnam, Mongolia, and Manchuria the standard is side aligned Oriental perspective.

The High Renaissance, Florence and Rome
The High Renaissance begins with Leonardo da Vinci who initially uses reduced scale center aligned fixed ego Renaissance prespective,. See *Adoration of the Magi*, 1481, Uffizi Gallery, Florence. For his *Last Supper*, begun 1498, *Sta. Maria dell Grazie*, Milan, Leonardo adopts reduced scale center aligned wide view fixed ego Renaissance perspective together with linear perspective. At the end of his life, Leonardo moves to France taking with him his I believe unfinished *Mona Lisa*, 1503 and the *Madonna and Child with St. Anne*, 1508, both in the Louvre. I see another hand finishing both paintings. The background landscape and the *Mona Lisa's* from her eyes up are based on Leonardo's reduced scale center aligned fixed ego wide-view Renaissance perspective. The out of scale nose, mouth with its famous "smile" and the figure below the eyes are based on standard French perspective, center aligned Semitic perspective. The same problem holds true with the *Madonna and Child and St. Anne*. The oversized head of St. Anne and the lamb-wrestling Jesus are based on center aligned Semitic perspective not Renaissance perspective.

Raffaello Santi is born in Urbino in 1483. The son of a painter he is a student of Perugino. Rafael's initial perspective is reduced scale center aligned fixed ego Renaissance perspective. See *Marriage of the Virgin*, 1504, Brera Gallery, Milan. By 1505 he is working in Florence and some four years later in Rome decorating a series of rooms in the Vatican. At this time his perspective is reduced scale center aligned fixed ego wide-view Renaissance perspective. See the *School of Athens*, 1508-11, Stanza della Signatura, the Vatican.

Michelangelo Buounarrati eight years the senior of Raphael is a Florentine. His *David*, 1501-4, Accademia, Florence, is based on reduced scale frontal aligned fixed ego Renaissance perspective. A *Wax of Maquette for the David*, in the Museum of Fine Arts, Boston, is based on this same perspective and is probably by Michelangelo. In 1508 Michelangelo is called to Rome to paint the *Sistine Ceiling*. The first half of the fresco is based on reduced scale, center aligned fixed ego Renaissance perspective. See the *Fall of man* and the *Expulsion*, 1510, the Vatican. After a brief respite Michelangelo finished the *Sistine Ceiling* using reduced scale center aligned fixed ego wide view Renaissance perspective. See the *Creation of Adam*, 1511. Raphael's use of a wide view in nearby rooms in the Vatican may have inspired the widening of Michelangelo's perspective. In 1513, Michelangelo adopts wide-view side aligned Hellenic perspective reduced scale forms. See *The Last Judgment*, 1534-41, Sistine Chapel, the Vatican. This change may have been inspired by Michelangelo's interest in the *Laocoon*, found in Rome in 1506, Vatican Museums, a Hellenic perspective work from Rhodes, based on reduced scale side aligned Hellenic perspective. Michelangelo will use Hellenic perspective the rest of his life including his designs for the new *St. Peter's*. These include the crossing and beyond, the *Dome* and the *Façade*. The standard Italian perspective *nave*, *Side Towers* and the central *Loggia of Benediction* are by Carlo Maderno. The Dome was executed after Michelangelo's death by Jaccomo della Porta is based on Micheangelo's wide view side aligned reduced scale Hellenic perspective. A lesser known aspect of Michelangelo'oevure are several pseudo antiquities by him. On the basis of style and perspective I find: the *Head of the Apollo Belvedere*, Vatican Museums, Rome, reduced scale center aligned Renaissance perspective; the *Head of the Medici Venus*, wide-view Renaissance perspective reduced scale forms in space, Uffiizi Gallery, Florence; the *Bartlet Head*, Museum of Fine Arts, Boston, wide-view Renaissance perspective, reduced scale to be by Michelangelo. I find that in antiquity reduced scale was used only in Egypt and North Africa. Two High Renaissance artists using, reduced scale center aligned Renaissance perspective are Fra Bartolomeo and Andrea del Sarto. See Fra Bartolomeo's *Vision of St. Bernard*, 1504-7, Accademia, Florence and Andrea del Sarto's *Madonna of the Harpies*, 1517, Uffizi Gallery,

Florence. Bramante the predecessor of Michelangelo as architect of St. Peter's uses reduced scale center aligned Renaissance perspective. See his *Tempieto*, 1502, Rome. Baldazarie Peruzzi uses Hellenic perspective, reduced scale center aligned. See *Frescos Villa Farnesina*, 1532, Rome.

The High Renaissance, Venice.
Giovanni Bellini dies in 1516. His Venetian successor Giorgione uses reduced scale fixed-ego Renaissance perspective, reduced scale forms in space. *Sleeping Venus*, ca. 1510, Painting Gallery, Dresden. The background landscape is by Titian. Titian uses wide-view, fixed ego Renaissance perspective, reduced scale forms in space. See *Bacchanal*, ca. 1517, Prado Museum, Madrid. The next generation of Venetian painters is lead by Tintorreto and Paolo Veronese. Tintorreto uses fixed ego Renaissance perspective, reduced scale forms in space. See *Miracle of the Slave*, 1548, Accademia, Venice. Veronese also uses fixed-ego Renaissance perspective, reduced scale forms in space. See *Feast in the House of Levi*, 1573, Accademia, Venice. The painter Lorenzo Lotto and the architect Palladio uses reduced scale center aligned Renaissance perspective. See Lotto's *Sacred Conversation*, 1520's, Kunsthistorisches Museum, Vienna and Palladio's *Villa Rotunda*, 1567-70, Vincenzo, Italy. El Greco, trained in Venice, uses standard Greek side aligned Hellenic perspective. See the *Burial of Count Orgaz*, 1586, S. Tome, Toledo. Corregio; active in Parma, uses fixed ego Semitic perspective, reduced scale forms in space. See *Jupiter and Io*, ca. 1532, Kunsthistoriches Museum, Vienna.

Mannerism.
Mannerism is the name given to the work of a group of sixteenth century Florentine artists and others of the generation following Michelangelo. The Mannerists give High Renaissance Classicism a twist by upsetting the classical balance between the natural and the abstract in favor of geometry. This produces emotionally charged works that are modernist or even postmodernist in they undermine classicism. Several of these artists used fixed ego reduced scale center aligned Semitic perspective, including: Pontormo, a pupil of Andrea del Sarto, see *Entombment*, ca. 1526, St. Felicia, Florence; Rosso Fiorentino, see *Descent from the Cross*, 1521, Communal Painting Gallery, Verona; Bronzino, a student

of Pontormo, see *Allegory of Venus*, ca. 1546, National Gallery, London and Parmigiano, see *Madonna of the Long Neck*, 1535, Uffizi Gallery, Florence. The under appreciated Guilio Romano's masterpiece the architecture and frescos of the *Villa del Te*, 1527-34, Mantua, is based on wide-view reduced scale center aligned Semitic perspective.

The Sixteenth Century in the North.
French and English art of the sixteenth century is in general based on Semitic perspective, center aligned France, side aligned England. The Netherlandish painter Peter Breugel the Elder uses wide-view center aligned Hellenic Perspective. See *Hunters in the Snow*, 1565, Kunsthistorishes Museum, Vienna. Germany enters the century using side aligned peripheral perspective. Albrecht Durer begins using side aligned peripheral perspective. See *Four Horsement*, woodcut, ca 1500. After a trip to Italy, 1494-5 Durer begins using side aligned Renaissance perspective. See *Adam and Eve*, engraving, 1504. Albert Altdorfer uses side aligned wide-view Renaissance perspective. See *The Battle of Issus*, 1529, Pinakotheck, Munich. Hans Holbein uses wide view center aligned Semitic perspective. See *Henry VIII*, 1540, National Gallery, Rome.

The Baroque in Italy.
Early in the seventeenth century there appears in Rome anti-Mannerist works that recapture some of the grandeur of the High Renaissance. At this time a number of major artists use a perspective other than the Italian standard perspective. Michelangelo inspires this direction. Michelangelo's successor as architect of *St. Peter's* is Giacomo della Porta who uses reduced scale center aligned Hellenistic perspective. See *Façade of Il Gesu*, 1575-1584, Rome. Della Porta's successor at *St. Peter's* is Carlo Maderno who uses standard Italian perspective, reduced scale center aligned Semitic perspective. The *Dome of St. Peter's*, completed by della Porta, 1590, is based on Michelangelo's reduced scale center aligned whide view Hellenic perspective. The *Façade of St. Peter's* also is based on Michelangelo's use of Hellenic perspective. The *Nave* west of the crossing, the *Flanking Towers* and the *Loggia of Benediction* are based on Moderno's standard Italian perspective. Maderno's successor at *St. Peter's* is the sculptor and architect, Gian Lorenzo Bernini. Bernini

uses reduced scale center aligned wide view Hellenic perspective. See his *Colonnade*, 1657, St. Peters Square and his *David*, 1632, Borghese Gallery, Rome. Bernini's contemporary, the architect Francesco Borromini uses reduced scale continuous center aligned Semitic perspective. See *S. Carlo alle Quarto Fontana*, 1638-57, Rome. The painter and architect, Pietro da Cortona, uses this same perspective. See *Rape of the Sabines*, 1628, Capitoline Museum, Rome. The architect, Flamino Ponzio uses wide view reduced scale center aligned Hellenic perspective. See the *Cappela Paolina*, 1605-11, S. Maria Maggiore, Rome. Two schools of painting launch on this new era. On one hand are the more classical Bolognese led by Annibale Carracci and on the other the revolutionary Caravaggio with his light and shadow "realism." Caravaggio uses wide-view reduced scale center aligned Semitic perspective. See *The Calling of St. Matthew*, 1599-1600, Contarelli Chapel, S. Luigi dei Francesi, Rome. Annibale Carracci uses reduced scale center aligned wide view fixed ego Renaissance perspective. See the *Farnese Gallery Ceiling Frescos*, 1597-1604, Rome. His cousin Lodovico Carracci uses reduced scale center aligned fixed ego Semitic perspective. See *The Holy Family with St. Francis*, 1591, Civic Museum, Centro, Italy. The Carracci school includes other important artists. Guido Rene uses reduced scale center aligned Renaissance perspective. See *Aurora Fresco*, 1613, Casino Rospigliosi, Rome. Domenicino uses wide-view center aligned reduced scale Semitic perspective. See *Last Communion of St. Jerome*, 1614, Vatican Museums. Guercino uses a wide-view fixed ego reduced scale center aligned Renaissance perspective to produce works of outstanding coherence. See *Aurora Fresco*, 1621-23, Villa Ludovisi, Rome. The peripatetic Luca Giordano uses reduced scale center aligned fixed-ego Semitic perspective for *Bachus and Ariadne*, 1685, Chrysler Museum, Norfolk, Va.

Seventeenth Century Flanders.
Standard Flemish perspective is center aligned Semitic perspective. Peter Paul Rubens uses center aligned wide-view Attic perspective. See *The Garden of Love*, 1638, the Louvre. Antony van Dyke uses center aligned fixed ego Attic perspective. See *Portrait of Charles II Hunting*, 1635, the Louvre.

Sixteenth and Seventeenth century France.

The art of the sixteenth century France is based on standard French perspective, center aligned Semitic perspective as is much French art of the seventeenth century. Exceptions include the architect Louis le Vau who uses center aligned wide-view Attic perspective. See *Chateau Vau-le-Vicomte*, 1657-61. The architect, Jules Haroudin-Mansart, uses center aligned wide view Hellenic perspective. See *Palace at Versailles*, 1669-1685. The etcher Jacques Calot uses center aligned wide view Semitic perspective. See his etchings *The Great Miseries of War*, 1653. Georges de la Tour also uses center aligned wide-view Semitic perspective. See *Joseph the Carpenter*, 1645, the Louvre. The Rome based French painter Nicholas Pousin uses center aligned wide-view fixed ego Hellenic perspective. See *Rape of the Sabines*, 1636-7, Metropolitan Museum of Art, New York City. Claude Lorraine, a painter of classical landscapes and resident of Rome uses center aligned wide-view Hellenic perspective. See *Sermon on the Mount*, 1650, Frick Collection, New York City. The painter Philipe de Champain uses center aligned Attic perspective. See *Mother Agnes and Sister Catherine*, 1662, the Louvre. The sculptor, Piere Puget, uses center aligned fixed ego Semitic perspective. See *Milo of Cortona*, 1671-82, the Louvre.

Seventeenth Century Dutch Painting.

The seventeenth century Netherlands produces a variety of distinguished artists working in a variety of genre. Many use standard Dutch perspective, center aligned Semitic perspective, but certain Dutch masters use other than this standard. The brilliant Frans Hals uses center aligned, wide-view, fixed-ego Hellenic perspective, forms in space. See *Women Regents of the Old Maids Home at Haarlem*, 1664, Frans Hals Museum, Haarlem. Rembrant uses side aligned wide-view Hellenic perspective, until ca 1661 when he turns to fixed-ego, side aligned wide-view Hellenic perspective. See *The Night Watch*, 1642, Rijksmuseum, Amsterdam and his fixed-ego *Return of the Prodigal Son*, ca. 1665, Hermitage Museum, St. Petersburg. I find that a large number of the works attributed to Rembrant, paintings, prints and drawings to not be based on Rembrant's side aligned wide view Hellenic perspective, but on standard Dutch perspective. Rembrant had some fifty pupils. It may be that he sold their work as his own, perhaps an excepted practice at the time, but still fraud. Seventeenth century Dutch artists not using standard Dutch perspective include Rembrant's pupil, Carel Fabritius who uses center aligned wide-view Semitic perspective. See *Linnet, 1654*, Mauritshuis, The Hague. Jan Vermeer uses center aligned wide view Hellenic perspective. See *Artist in His Studio*, ca. 1665, Art History Museum, Vienna. *Girl with a Pearl Earring*, 1665, Maritshius, The Hague, I find based on standard Flemish/Dutch perspective and may be the work of Michiel Sweerts. Gerard ter Borch uses center aligned wide-view Semitic perspective. See *Portrait of Hellen van der Schalhe as a Child*, 1644, Rijksmuseum, Amsterdam. Pieter de Hooch uses center aligned fixed-ego Semitic perspective. See *Bedroom*, ca. 1669, National Gallery of Art, Washington DC. Gabriel Metsu uses center aligned Hellenic perspective. See *The Sick Child*, 1660, the Rijksmuseum, Amsterdam. The landscape painter Jan van Goyen uses center aligned wide view Semitic perspective. See *River Scene*, 1636, Fogg Art Museum, Cambridge, Mass. Salomon can Ruysdael uses center aligned wide view Semitic perspective. See *Windmill Near Wijh*, ca. 1665, Ryksmuseum, Amsterdam. Meyndhart Hobbem uses center aligned wide view Semitic perspective. See *Avenue at Middelharnis*, 1668, National Gallery, London. The still life painter Willem Kalf uses center aligned Hellenic perspective. See *Still Life with Nautilus Cup*, ca. 1660, Private Collection.

Seventeenth Century Spanish Art.
Standard Spanish perspective beginning in the eleventh century is bottom aligned frontal perspective, reduced scale forms. El Greco the Greek use center aligned wide view Hellenic perspective. See the *Burial of Count Orgaz*, 1586, S. Tome, Toledo. Diego Velazquez uses center aligned reduced scale wide-view Semitic perspective with disconnected forms. See the *Maids of Honor*, 1656, the Prado Museum, Madrid, not the mysterious work often described, but a some what informal portrait of Princess Margarita seen in the center in group of her retainers. Francisco Ribalta uses reduced scale, bottom aligned wide view Semitic perspective. See *St. Francis Embracing Christ on the Cross*, ca. 1620. Provincial Museum, Valencia. The sculptor Gregorio Fernandez uses wide-view bottom aligned reduced scale Semitic perspective. See *St. Bruno*, 1634,

Valladolid Museum. The painter, Juisepe de Ribera, uses reduced scale center aligned Renaissance perspective. See the *Martyrdom of St. Francis Bartholmeiu*, 1630, Prado Museum, Madrid. Estaban Murillo also uses reduced scale center aligned Renaissance perspective. See the *Rest in the Flight into Egypt*, 1645, Detroit Art Institute.

Eighteenth Century Italian Art
With eighteenth century Italian art the continuing standard is reduced scale center aligned Semitic perspective. Gianbattista Tiepolo uses, reduced scale center aligned Renaissance perspective. See *Decorations of the Kaisersaal*, 1752, the Residence, Wurzburg, Germany. His brilliant son, Gian Domenica Tiepolo uses a wide-view fixed ego reduced scale center aligned Hellenic perspective,. See the *Villa Volmarana Frescos*, 1757, Vincenza, Italy. Landscapes featuring architecture, vedutas, are an important eighteenth century genre. Francesco Gaudi uses wide view fixed-ego reduced scale center aligned Hellenic perspective. See *Santa Maria della Salute*, ca. 1740, Ca' d' Oro, Venice. Canaletto uses wide-view reduced scale center aligned Hellenic perspective,. See *Basin of St. Marco*, 1730, Museum of Fine Arts, Boston.

Eighteen Century French Art.
Standard French perspective, center aligned Semitic perspective continues to prevail during the eighteenth century. Antoine Watteau uses wide-view center aligned Semitic perspective. See the *Embarkation for Cythera*, ca. 1717, the Louvre. Francois Boucher uses center aligned Renaissance perspective. See *Rest on the Flight into Egypt*, 1765, Museum of Fine Arts, Boston. Jean-Honore Fragonard uses center aligned wide-view Renaissance perspective. See *The Swing*, 1767, Wallace Collection, London. Jean-Baptiste-Simeon Chardin uses fixed-ego center aligned Hellenic perspective. See *The Benediction*, 1740, the Louvre. Jean-Baptise Greuze uses wide-view center aligned Semitic perspective. See the *Village Bride*, 1761, the Louvre. Hubert Robert uses center aligned Renaissance perspective. See *Demolition of Houses*, 1786-88, Carnavalet Museum, Paris. The sculptor Jean-Antoine Houdon uses center aligned Renaissance perspective. See *George Washington*, 1788-92, State Capitol,

Richmond, Va. The architect Jaques-Ange Gabriel uses wide view center aligned Semitic perspective. See the *Petit Trianon*, 1762-68, Versailles.

Eighteenth Century German Art.
Standard German perspective beginning in the sixteenth century is side aligned Semitic perspective, Johaun Fisher van Erlach uses fixed ego side aligned Semitic perspective. See the *Karleskirche*, begun 1715, Vienna. The architect Lucas von Hildebrandt uses wide view side aligned Hellenic perspective. See *Upper Belvedere Palace*, 1721-24, Vienna. The French architect, active in Germany, Francoise de Cuvillies uses fixed ego center aligned Semitic perspective. See the *Amalienburge*, 1734-39, near Munich. The sculptor Ignaz Gunter uses wide view side aligned Semitic perspective. See the *Guardian Angel*, 1763, Burgersaal, Munich.

Eighteen Century English and American Art.
Standard English perspective since the thirteenth century is side aligned Semitic perspective which also becomes the standard in North America. There is a survival in the seventeenth century English vernacular art and side aligned peripheral perspective in England and the English colonies of North America. See *Mrs. Freake and Baby Mary*, 1674, Worcester Art Museum, Massachusetts. Native American art is based in side aligned Oriental perspective space. See *War Helmut*, nineteenth century, from south east Alaska, American Museum of Natural History. The leading English architects of the seventeenth century and eighteenth century use standard English perspective. The painter Joshua Reynolds uses side aligned Attic perspective. See *Mrs. Siddons as the Tragic Muse*, 1784, Huntington Gallery, San Marino, Ca. Thomas Gainsborough uses wide view Hellenic perspective, forms not in space. See *Mrs. Siddonds*, 1785, National Gallery, London. The American colonial painters Benjamin West and John Singleton Copley use side aligned Hellenic perspective. See West's *Death of Wolf*, 1770, National Gallery of Canada, Ottawa and Copley's *Watson and the Shark*, 1778, National Gallery of Art, Washington, D.C. The American Gilbert Stuart uses this same perspective, see *Mrs. Richard Yates*, 1793, Worcester Art Museum, Massachusetts.

Neoclassicism
The modern age begins in Western Europe and North America during the second half of the eighteen century with dramatic philosophical, political, social and industrial change are all which are reflected in the visual arts. At this time the Greek Classical style is rediscovered. However Neoclassicism is not a revival a break with the classical tradition. Beginning in the Renaissance on the Classical style had been an essential ingredient of European art. The idealized human figure, the classical orders functioning in a sort of three-dimensional grid, along with a balanced blend of the natural and the abstract, a hierarchy of form and the subjects of major works derived from literature. In the second half of the eighteenth century a system I call surface design, line and pattern that organized the composition two-dimensionally rather than three-dimensional solids, the classical practice. This change spreads through the visual arts while at the same time national standard perspective continues. Anton Raphael Mengs uses side aligned Renaissance perspective. See *Parnassus*, 1761, Villa Albani, Rome. Antonio Canova uses reduced scale center aligned Renaissance perspective,. See *Pauline Broghese as Venus*, 1808, Borghese Gallery, Rome. In both cases surface design prevails. The works of the Great Spanish painter Francisco Goya owes a little to Neoclassicism. His works are classical in the use of powerful three dimensional forms but the forms are disconnected and the subject matter is often revolutionary. Goya, uses wide view reduced scale center aligned disconnect Attic perspective that gives his images an immediacy. See *The Third of May*, 1808, 1814-15, the Prado Museum, Madrid. The overriding influence of surface design is seen in the work of Jaques-Louis David. David uses wide view center aligned Attic perspective. See the *Oath of the Horatii*, 1784, the Louvre Museum. His follower Pierce-Paul Prud'hon uses wide view center aligned Renaissance perspective. See *The Empress Josephine*, 1808, the Louvre. The more romantic, Antoine-Jean Gross uses center aligned Hellenistic perspective. See *Napoleon in the Pest House at Jaffa*, 1804, the Louvre Museum. The great English poet painter William Blake uses wide view side aligned peripheral perspective. See *Illustrations for Paradise Lost*, 1795, Tate Gallery, London. The Neoclassical style is called the Federal style in the new United States. The architecture of

Thomas Jefferson stands out because of his use of fixed ego side aligned Semitic perspective. See Monticello, 1770-1806, Carlotteville, VA. Jefferson's protégé Benjamin Latrobe, uses center aligned wide view Semitic perspective, see Baltimore Cathedral, 1805.

Romanticism and Realism
During the nineteenth century Neoclassicism, Romanticism and Realism coexist in Europe and North America, but in time Romanticism and Realism come to dominate. The Neoclassic style involves style and subject matter drawn from Antiquity. Line defines composition. Romanticism is more diverse. There is much more variety in subject matter, an emphasis on emotion, non classical and exotic styles are imitated and paint is applied variously while surface design continues. Realism rejects Antiquity and turns to nature and contemporary life. Surface design continues while individualism is on the rise. Landscape and the observation of nature are all important as is color and the inventive application of paint. The Neoclassicist, Jean Auguste-Dominique Ingres' precisely painted works become Romantic in time. Ingres uses wide-view center aligned Hellenic perspective. See *Odalisque*, 1814, the Louvre. Theodore Gericault, a Romantic, uses wide-view center aligned Semitic perspective. See the *Raft of the Medusa*, 1818-19, the Louvre. Eugene Delacoix, a leading Romantic is famous for the richness of his color. He uses wide-view center aligned Attic perspective. See the *Massacre of Chios*, 1822-24, the Louvre. Gustave Courbet is the leading Realist. His subject include landscape, heroisized everyday life and the figure. Courbet explores a textured use of paint in works based on wide-view center aligned Semitic perspective. See *Burial at Ornans*, 1849-50. Honore Daumier, primarily a graphic artist, satirically distances himself from classical idealism. Daumier uses wide-view center aligned Hellenic perspective. See the *Third Class Carriage*, 1863-65, Metropolitan Museum of Art, New York City. Ernst Messonier uses wide-view center aligned Semitic perspective for subjects taken from contemporary history. See the *Barricades*, 1849, the Louvre. The sculpture Francois Rude uses wide view center aligned Semitic perspective. See *The Marseillaises*, 1833-36, *Arch of Triumph*, Paris. The sculptor Antione Louis Barye, famous for animals, uses center aligned Hellenic perspective. See *Jaguar Devouring a Hare*, 1850-9,

the Louvre. The innovative architect Henri Labrouste uses fixed-ego center aligned Semitic perspective. See the *Ste. Genevieve Library*, 1843-50, Paris. From later in the century comes the medieval revival architect Viollet-le-Duc who uses center aligned Hellenic perspective. See *Tomb of Duc de Morny*, 1865, Paris. The Barbizon school of French landscape painters pioneers out door painting. Theodore Rousseau uses center aligned Attic perspective. See *Under Birches*, 1843-43, Toledo Ohio Museum of Art. Francois Millet, a painter of heroic peasants and landscape, uses wide-view Hellenic perspective. See *The Gleaners*, 1857, the Louvre. The figure and landscape painter Camille Corot uses center aligned fixed ego Semitic perspective. See his romantic landscape, *Memory of Montefontaine*, 1864, the Louvre. Thomas Couture, the teacher of Edouard Manet, uses disconnected center aligned Attic perspective. See *Romans of the Decadence*, 1847, The Louvre.

There is an outburst of creativity in the arts during the nineteenth century in Germany. Caspar David Friedrich uses wide view side aligned Hellenic perspective for his precisely painted landscapes. See *Abbey in an Oak Forest*, 1804-10, National Museum, Berlin. Phillipe Otto Runge uses wide-view side aligned Semitic perspective. See *Hulsenbech Children*, 1805-6, Kunst Halle, Hamburg. The Romantic Karl Blechen uses wide view Semitic perspective, forms not in space. See *Women Bathing in the Gardens at Tivoli*, 1830s. National Museum, Berlin. The Austrian Landscape painter Ferdinand George Waldmuller uses side aligned fixed ego Renaissance perspective,. See *View of the Halslattersee*, 1838, History Museum, Vienna. From later in the century comes the genre and history painter, Adolph von Menzel who uses side aligned wide-view Semitic perspective. See the *Artist's Sister with a Candle*, 1897, Bavarian State Collection, Munich. The figure painter, Hans von Marees, uses side aligned wide view Semitic perspective. See *The Hesperides*, 1857, New Pinakothech, Munich. The sculptor Daniel Rauch uses side aligned fixed ego Semitic perspective. See *Equestrian Monument of Frederich the Great*, 1836-51, Berlin. The architect Friedrich Schinkel uses side aligned Attic perspective, for his neoclassical *Old Museum*, 1824-30, Berlin.

The nineteenth century is the great age of English landscape painting. Joseph Mallord Turner uses side aligned fixed-ego Semitic perspective. See *Slave Ship*, 1840, Museum of Fine Arts, Boston. John

Constable use side aligned wide-view Semitic perspective. See *The Haywain*, 1821, National Gallery, London. Richard Parks Bonnington uses side aligned Hellenic perspective. See the *Park at Versailles*, ca. 1822, the Louvre. In the mid nineteenth century the English Pre-Raphaelites, a group dedicated to reform in the arts, use styles inspired by the Early Renaissance and a meticulous observation of nature to explore history and everyday life. John Everest Millais stands with his use of side aligned wide view Hellenic perspective. See *Christ in the House of His Parents*, 1850, Tate Gallery, London, fictional history and everyday life. The eccentric Richard Dadd uses side aligned Hellenic perspective. See *The Ferry Feller's Master Stroke*, 1858-64, Tate Gallery, London. The architect Phillip Webb uses side aligned wide-view Semitic perspective. See *Red Horse*, 1859, Rent. The architect William Butterfield uses side aligned Hellenic perspective. See *Keble College*, 1873-6, Oxford.

American art starts to come to the fore during the nineteenth century. The standard perspective is side aligned Semitic perspective. The landscape painter Frederich Church uses side aligned Renaissance perspective. See *Cotopaxi*, 1862, Private Collection. The German born and trained Albert Bierstadt uses side aligned Renaissance perspective. See *Rocky Mountains*, 1863. Metropolitan Museum of Art, New York City. William Sidney Mount uses side aligned fixed-ego Semitic perspective. See *The Power of Music*, 1847, Cleveland Museum of Art. The landscape painter, George Innes uses side aligned Renaissance perspective. See *Lackawanna Valley*, 1855, National Gallery of Art, Washington, DC. James Abbot McNiel Whistle uses side aligned wide-view Semitic perspective. See *Symphony in White, Number Two*, 1864, Tate Gallery, London. John Singer Sargeant uses side aligned fixed-ego frontal perspective, forms not in space. See *The Boit Daughters*, 1882, Museum if Fine Arts, Boston. Windslow Hommer uses side aligned Attic perspective. See *Snap the Whip*, 1872, Butler Institute, Youngstown, Ohio. Thomas Eakins uses side aligned fixed-ego Attic perspective. See *The Gross Clinic*, 1875, Philadelphia Museum of Art. Albert Pinkham Ryder uses side aligned wide-view Hellenic perspective,. See *Siegfried and the Rhine Maidens*, 1888-91, National Gallery of Art, Washington, D.C. The sculptor Augustus Saint Gauden uses side aligned wide-view Hellenic perspective. See *Shaw Memorial*, 1884-97, Boston. The sculptor, Daniel Chester French, uses side aligned Hellenic perspective. See *Minute Man, 1873-74*, Concord, Mass. The architect Henry Hobson Richardson use side aligned wide-view Hellenic perspective. See *Marshall Field Warehouse*, 1885-87, destroyed, Chicago, Illinois. The Philadelphia architect Frank Furness uses side aligned fixed-ego Semitic perspective, forms not in space. See *Pennsylvania Academy of Fine Arts*, 1871-76, Philadelphia, Pa.

Impressionism.

Impressionism is a new style that is unlike anything before. It is radical in color and application of paint. Impressionism arises out of Courbet, the French Barbizon school of open air painting and the work of Edouard Manet. The first group show is in 1874. Loosely applied separate strokes of paint that vary in color interact visually to capture the effects of color and light as seen in nature. Still life, everyday life, sometimes figures and the landscape above all subjects. Open-air painting is a way of life for a number of leading artist's who use perspectives that produce coherent works of art. The Edouard Manet, a brilliant colorist, in time becomes more of an Impressionist. Manet uses center aligned wide view disconnected Attic perspective. See the *Luncheon*, 1863, The Louvre. Paul Cézanne, sometimes a member of the group, will bestride both Impressionism and Post Impressionism, see below. The core of the Impressionists group are Claude Monet, Camille Pissaro, Pierre-Auguste Renoir, Alfred Sisley, Edgar Degas, Berth Morisot, Frederich Bazille (killed in the Franco Prussian war) and the painter and collector Gustave Caillebotte. Monet use center aligned fixed-ego Attic perspective. After 1900 he will use center aligned wide-view Hellenic perspective. See his Attic perspective *Bridge at Argenteuil*, 1874 d'Orsay Museum, Paris, and his Hellenic perspective *Clouds*, 1916-26, Orangerie Museum, Paris. Camille Pissaro uses center aligned fixed-ego Semitic perspective. See *Red Roofs*, 1877, d'Orsay Museum, Paris. The English Alfred Sisley uses side aligned wide-view fixed-ego Attic perspective. See *Flood at Marly*, 1876, d'Orsay Museum, Paris. Renoir, uses center aligned wide-view, fixed-ego Hellenic perspective. See *Moulin de la Galette*, 1876, d'Orsay Museum. Edgar Degas, uses center aligned wide-view Hellenic perspective. See L'Absinthe, 1876, d'Orsay Museum. Berthe Morisot also uses wide-view Hellenic perspective. See *Summer Scene,*

Bathers, Fogg Museum, Cambridge, Massachusetts. Gustave Caillebotte uses disconnected center aligned oriental perspective. See *Paris Street Scene, Rainy weather*, 1877, Art Institute Chicago. The America Mary Cassatt uses continuous side aligned Semitic perspective. The German Impressionist Max Leberman uses side aligned Renaissance perspective. See *Dutch Sewing School*, 1876, Van der Heydt Museum, Wuppertal, Germany. The sculptor, August Rodin, associated with Impressionism, uses center aligned wide-view Hellenic perspective. See *Burgers of Calais*, 1886, Calais, France.

Post Impressionism.
There are four major Post Impressionists; Georges Seurat, Vincent van Gogh, Paul Gauguin and Paul Cézanne. Each has very individual in style, that radically departs from Impressionism and each uses a different perspective. The French Seurat's dot like strokes regularizes impressionism. Seurat uses center aligned fixed-ego Semitic perspective. See *Sunday Afternoon on the Grand Jette*, 1884-86, The Art Institute Chicago. Seurat's follower, Paul Signac uses center aligned fixed-ego Semitic perspective. See *Portrait of M. Felix Feneon*, 1890, Private Collection. The Dutch Vincent van Gogh uses center aligned disconnected wide view Attic perspective. See the *Night Cafe*, 1888, Yale University Art Gallery, New Haven, Conn. The French Paul Gauguin begins as an impressionist, but moves to a style based on a pattern of richly colored shapes using standard French perspective center aligned Semiotic perspective. Then in 1889 after seeing art from Java at the Paris Worlds Fair he begins using center aligned wide-view peripheral perspective. In 1991, Gauguin moves to Tahiti. See *Ia Orana Maria*, 1891, Metropolitan Museum of Art, New York City. Mysteriously from time to time he reverts to standard French perspective.

Cézanne
Paul Cézanne is both the most conservative and radical of the Post Impressionists. Cézanne use a unique perspective that comes naturally to him. He begins with a wide-view Oriental perspective. In this context he sees individual as nonaligned and then individually center aligned with a large ego. Cézanne's work has a history of first being ridiculed as

incompetent and later as naïve and praised as individual, creative and for the same supposed perspective "inconsistencies". Tragically I find that some eighty of Cézanne's paintings including major works altered in most cases by frontal perspective outlines. In ca 1885 Cézanne modified his perspective by fixing his ego, See his *Turn in the Road*, 1879-82, Museum of Fine Arts, Boston and his fixed ego, *The large Bathers*, 1906, Philadelphia. Museum of Art.

Late Nineteenth Century Art.
During the late nineteenth and early twentieth century there appears in Europe a new style called among other things Art Nouveau. Art Nouveau typically involves curving lines and a strong surface design. It is manifested in painting, sculpture, architecture and the decorative arts. The Barcelona architect, Antonio Gaudi uses bottom aligned reduced scale wide view Hellenic perspective. See the *Casa Mila*, 1905, Barcelona. The Belgium architect Victor Horta uses center aligned fixed-ego Semitic perspective. See *Tassel House*, 1892-93, Brussels. The American architect Louis Sullivan, uses side aligned Hellenic perspective. See the *Guaranty Trust Building*, 1894-95, Buffalo, New York. Henry Toulouse Lautrect uses center aligned wide-view Hellenic perspective. See his poster, *Jane Avril*, 1899. The Norwegian painter, Edvard Munch, uses side aligned Hellenic perspective. See *The Dance of Life*, 1900, National Gallery, Oslo. The two leading members of a group of French artists called the Nabis, Prophets, are Edouard Vuillard and Pierre Bonnard. Vuillard uses center aligned wide-view frontal perspective. See *The Workroom*, 1893, Smith College Museum of Art, Northampton, Mass. Bonnard uses center aligned wide view Semitic perspective. See his lithograph, *Nursemaids*, 1899. The French sculptor Aristide Maillol uses center aligned Hellenic perspective. See *Night*, 1902, Art Museum, Winterthur, Switzerland. The Symbolist Achille Redon uses center aligned Hellenic perspective. See his lithograph, *Marsh Flower*, 1885. The Belgium James Ensor uses center aligned wide-view Hellenic perspective, forms in space. See *The Entry of Christ into Brussels*, 1888, Private Collection.

The Fauves

From early in the twentieth century comes a group of French painters called the Fauves, wild beasts. Their freely painted, brightly colored works were inspired by Gauguin and van Gogh. Maurice Vlamink and Raoul Dufy use standard French perspective, center aligned Semitic perspective. Andre Derain uses standard French perspective until sometime in 1906 when he turns to center aligned peripheral perspective. See his Semitic perspective, *London Bridge*, 1906, Museum of Modern Art, New York City and his peripheral perspective, *Turning Road*, 1906, Museum of Fine Arts, Houston. Georges Rouault uses center aligned wide-view Semitic perspective. See *Old King*, 1916, Carnegie Museum, Pittsburgh, Pa. Georges Braque a future cubist as a Fauve uses a narrowly center aligned large ego aligned. See *Boats on Beach*, 1906, Los Angeles County Museum. Henri Matisse uses a center aligned wide view Hellenic perspective, until 1904-5 when he invents the first of two new perspectives. See his Hellenic perspective *Carmelina*, 1903, Museum of Fine Arts, Boston. The "primitive" Henri Rousseau, not a Fauve, uses center aligned wide-view Semitic perspective. See *Sleeping Gypsy*, 1897, Museum of Modern Art, New York City.

Mtisse Perspectives

Henri Matisse begins using center aligned wide view Hellenic perspective. In 1904-5, perhaps after seeing Cézanne paintings at the 1904 Autumn Salon, Paris, he introduces a perspective that begins with a wide view and then sees individual forms nonaligned. This perspective is similar to Oceanic perspective which lacks a fixed-ego. See *Le Bonheur de Vivre*, 1905-6, Barnes Foundation, Philadelphia, Pa. In 1907 Matisse introduces second new perspective. Individual forms are seen as nonaligned in the context of center wide view Hellenic perspective. Again See *Blue Nude, Memory of Briska*, 1907, the Baltimore Museum of Art. Matisse will use these two perspectives alternately for the rest of his life. Matisse's forms are finally seen nonaligned while Cézanne's are finally seen aligned with the large ego.

Picasso's Perspectives

During his lifetime Pablo Picasso used thirteen different perspectives twelve of which he invented. He began with reduced scale forms first seen nonaligned and then bottom aligned with a small fixed ego aligned to the bottom center of the picture, perspective No. One. See *Moulin de la Galette*, Paris 1900, Guggenheim Museum, New York City. The fixed ego reduced scale are central Picasso's perspectives. In the fall of 1901 after seeing woodcuts by Paul Gauguin Picasso adopts perspective No. Two, a peripheral perspective. A fixed small ego is aligned to a point at the bottom left side to the of a picture. Reduced scale forms are first seen nonaligned and then successively seen peripherally aligned to the small fixed ego bottom left. Picasso's No Two forms are seen in continuous space and appear touchable. Picasso uses Two for his Blue and Rose periods, 1901-1906. See the *Blind Man's Meal*, 1903, Metropolitan Museum of Art, New York City. In the fall of 1906 Picasso introduced perspective No. Three which is the sane as Two except the ego is now large. Picasso uses this third perspective for dramatic differences in color and scale between shapes. See *Two Nudes*, 1906, Museum of Modern Art, New York City. In May 1907 Picasso introduces perspective No. Four. Four aligns a fixed large ego to the bottom center of the picture placed close to the picture surface. Reduced scale shapes first seen nonaligned are sequentially seen bottom aligned to the fixed visual ego. The flatten shapes are cut out by unaligned dark areas and lines. This Picasso persecutive is complex, but works composed this way seen correctly spring readily to life. The first version of the *Les Demoiselles d'Avignon*, begun in the spring of 1907, Museum of Modern Art, New York City was based on Four. Now only the central two figures and the gray background curtain are based on Four. In the summer of 1907 Picasso using perspective No. Five begins repainting the *Les Demoiselles d'Avignon*. Five is the same as Four except the ego is now small. Today only the figures on the right, the still life on a table and blue background curtains are based in Five. Dark outlines and contiguous darks carve out the two figures on the right who's mask like faces were inspired by African and Oceanic art. African Oceanic art however are based on perspectives other than Picasso's. In the spring of 1908 Picasso uses perspective No. Six to repaint the woman pushing back a brown curtain on the left. With Six a bottom center fixed ego close to the picture surface is aligned to point behind the picture surface. With Six reduced scale forms are first seen nonaligned. Today *Les Demoiselles d'Avignon* stands out because of its radical appearance and as the product of three unique perspectives. I find that all five "Demoiselles" including the mask like faces on the right correctly seen have the face of Picasso's companion Fernand Olivier laying to rest the idea that the painting is about sex or disease or that it denigrates women. For me the five monumental women rise up to celebrate womanhood and the beautiful Fernand. In summer 1908 perspective No. Seven appears. Seven is like Six except the ego is large. See *Landscape, Rue des Bois*, 1908, Museum of Modern Art, New York. In the fall of 1909 Picasso introduces perspective No. Eight. With Eight the fixed bottom aligned small ego is aligned to reduced scale surfaces rather than shapes. These surfaces are first seen nonaligned with the divisions between shapes remaining nonaligned. See *Still Life with a Liquer Bottle*, 1909, Museum of Modern Art, New York City. In the fall of 1910 using perspective No. Nine Picasso repaints some his summer perspective Eight works. Nine uses a bottom center fixed ego alined to a point behind the picture surface. The dark lines that separate shapes remain nonaligned while the reduced scale surfaces are bottom aligned to the large ego fixed at the bottom center of the picture. Perspective nine slices out shapes with each seen in a separate space. The result is the extraordinary dream like works of the so called "hermetic period". See *Ma Jolie*, 1911, the Museum of Modern Art, New York City, which contains "secret" portraits of Picasso and his beloved companion Eva. In the spring of 1912 Picasso introduces perspective No. Ten. With Ten the fixed small ego is aligned to a bottom center to point on the picture surface rather than behind. Reduced scale surfaces are first seen nonaligned and the bottom aligned with the small fixed bottom ego. At this time Picasso begins using collage a natural adjunct to works composed of shapes seemingly cut from the picture surface. See *Still Life with Chair Canning*, 1912, Picasso Museum, Paris. He will use Ten through the summer of 1912. That fall he repaints some of his summer 1912 pictures using perspective No. Eleven. Eleven is the same as Ten except the bottom center fixed ego is now large. See *Man with a Hat*, a self portrait drawing with collage and painted elements, 1912, Museum of Modern Art, New York City. Picasso uses Eleven until the spring of 1912 when he returns to Ten. He will use Ten and Eleven alternately for the next fifty years. He uses Eleven for six periods, 1912-1914, 1915-1917, 1921-1923, 1938-1941, ca. 1944-1947 and from 1965 to his death.

Cubism

The term Cubism is first used in 1908 in reference to of works by Georges Braque. Braque center aligned narrow Oriental perspective until 1908. See *Viaduct at L'estaque*, 1907, the Minneapolis Institute of Arts. After visiting Picasso's studio Braque begins seeing forms nonaligned before narrow center aligning them with a large ego. See *House at L'estaque*, 1908, Art Museum, Basel. The French Cubists Fernando Leger and Robert Delaunay center aligned forms first seen nonaligned and then with the small Semitic perspective ego followed. See Leger's *The City*, 1919, Philadelphia Museum of Art and Robert Delaunay's *Eiffel Tower*, 1910, Guggenheim Museum, New York City. The Catalan Juan Gris uses the bottom aligned small Semitic ego to forms first seen nonaligned. Gris's collage, *Breakfast*, 1914, Museum of Modern Art, New York City. The French cubist, Jean Metzinger uses center aligned fixed ego Semitic perspective. See *Guitar and Clarinet*, 1920, Hirshhorn Museum, Washington, D.C. The sculptor and brother of Marcel Duchamp, Raymond Duchamp-Villon uses center aligned wide view Semitic perspective. See *Horse*, 1914, Philadelphia Museum.

German Expressionism

Early Modernism in Germany is influenced by Post Impressionism and Cubism. Paula Moderson uses side aligned Hellinic perspective. See *Self Portrait with Camelia Branch*, 1907, Folkwang Museum, Essen. The colorist Emil Nolde uses the same perspective Moderson. See *The Last Supper*, 1909, State Museum for Art, Copenhagen. In Dresden and then Berlin there is a group of modern artists called the Bridge which includes Ernst Ludwig Kirchner, Emil Heckel, Max Peckstein, and Karl Schmidt-Rottluff. In Munich another German Expressionist group, the Blue Rider, includes the Russian abstractionist Vasily Kandindsky, the Russian Alex von Jawlensky and the Germans Franz Mark, August Macke, Lionel Feiniger, Gabriel Munter and the unique Swiss painter,

Paul Klee. Kirchner uses side aligned peripheral perspective, until around 1913 when he turns to side aligned Semitic perspective. See Kirchner's peripheral perspective, *Street Dresden*, 1908, and his frontal perspective, *Street Berlin*, 1913, both in the Museum of Modern Art, New York City. Erich Heckel uses side aligned peripheral perspective. See Heckel's *Two Men at a Table*, 1912, Kunsthalle, Essen. Peripheral perspective represents these artists returning to German roots. Max Peckstein also uses side aligned peripheral perspective. See *Indian and Woman*, 1910, Saint Louis Art Museum. Franz Mark uses side aligned peripheral perspective. See *Large Blue Horses*, 1911, Walker Art Center, Minneapolis, Minnesota. August Macke uses side aligned Hellenic perspective. See *Great Zoological Garden*, 1912, Museum an Ostwold, Dortmund. The German sculptor Wilhelm Lehmbruch, uses side aligned wide-view peripheral perspective. See *Standing Youth*, 1913, Museum of Modern Art, New York City. Vasily Kandinsky uses side aligned wide-view frontal perspective. See *Sketch for Composition II*, 1909-10. Guggengheim Museum, New York City.

Futurism
In 1909-10 inspired by the Italian Poet Filippo Tommaso Marrinetti's call for a revolutionary new art a group of Italian artists, the Futurists, Umberto Boccioni, Carlo Cara, Luigi Russolo, Gino Severini and Giacomo Balla begin a pursuit of this idea. In October 1911, Boccioni and Cara went to Paris to meet with Severini and witness Cubism first hand. The Futurists use standard Italian perspective, center aligned reduced scale Semitic perspective with the exception of Balla, who uses center aligned reduced scale fixed-ego Semitic perspective. See *Dynamism of a Dog on a Leash*, 1912, Albright-Knox Gallery, Buffalo, New York City.

De Style
During World I, a group of artists in the Netherlands form the De Stijl group. They use Dutch standard perspective, center aligned Semitic perspective, except for their outstanding member, Piet Mondrian. Mondrian begins using standard Dutch perspective, see *Mill by the Water*, 1912, Museum of Modern Art, New York. In 1913-14, working in Paris and under the influence of Cubism, he adopts center aligned peripheral

perspective. See *Broadway Boogie-Woogie*, 1942-43, Museum of Modern Art, New York City, painted in New York City during World War II.

Russian Modernism
Modernism in Russia is led by a group of Moscow artists that emerge in the twenties. Most use standard Russian perspective, side aligned Semitic perspective. Alexander Rodochenko, a sculptor, painter and photographer, uses a wide-view side aligned Semitic perspective. See his wide view photograph, *Assembling For The Demonstration*, 1928. Kasimir Malivich uses side aligned Semitic perspective. See his *Supremacist Composition, White on White*, 1918, Museum of Modern Art, New York City, Lyubon Popova a pioneer of Russian Modernism uses side aligned fixed-ego Semitic perspective. See *Early Morning*, 1914, Museum of Modern Art, New York City.

Modern Architecture
Modern Architecture grows from the work of such late nineteenth century architects as the Americans Henry Hobson Richardson, Louis Sullivan and Frank Lloyd Wright. Wright uses side aligned wide-view Oriental perspective. See Wright's *Robie House*, 1909, Chicago. After World War I Modern architecture develops in Europe. This is lead by the Dutch architect Gerrit Rietveld using standard Dutch perspective, center aligned Semitic perspective. See *Schroder House*, 1924, Utrecht. The German architect Walter Gropius uses side aligned fixed-ego Semitic perspective. See *Baushaus Buildings*, 1925-26. Dessau, Germany. Meis van der Roh also uses side aligned fixed-ego Semitic perspective. See *Spanish Pavilion*, 1937, Barcelona. The German-Jewish architect Erich Mendelson designs his *Einstein Towe*r 1920-21, Potsdam, Germany, in a style reminiscent if Art Nouveau using side aligned wide-view Oriental perspective. The French/Swiss architect Le Corbusier uses center aligned wide-view Semitic perspective, forms in space. See *Villa Savoye*, 1929-30, Poissy-sur-Seine. The Italian Giuseppe Terragni uses reduced scale center aligned Hellenic perspective. See *House of The People*, 1923-26, Como, Italy. The American, Raymond Hood uses side aligned fixed-ego Semitic perspective. See *Magraw Hill Building*, 1931, New York City. The Brazilian Oscar Niemeyer uses side aligned Oriental

perspective the South American standard perspective. See *Palace of The Dawn*, 1959, Brasilia. The English architect, James Stirling, uses side aligned wide-view Semitic perspective. See *History Faculty*, 1968, Cambridge, England. The American Richard Meier uses side aligned fixed ego Semitic perspective. See *Douglas House*, 1971-3, Harbor Springs Michigan. Side aligned fixed ego Semitic perspective is also used by the American architect Louis Kahn. See *Kimbal Art Museum*, 1972, Forth Worth, Texas. The Chinese American Leoh Ming Peo, uses side aligned wide view Oriental perspective. See the *Louvre Pyramid*, 1988, Paris.

Photography.
The camera is a machine that by itself can not make a work of art. The focal point of the lens is not a visual ego. However, a photographer using a view finder and a particular visual ego can compose a photograph that depends on a particular use of the visual ego that is a work of art. Still like nature photographs can be beautiful can be beau. Photography is invented in the first half of the nineteenth century. See Jacques Daguerr's daguerreotype, *Boulevard de Temple*, ca. 1838, National Museum, Munich, the buildings and boulevard are based in center aligned Semitic perspective but the composition is not. A circle of American photographers around Alfred Stieglits, launches Modern Photography in the United States. Stieglitz uses side aligned wide-view Hellenic perspective. See *The Steerage*, 1907. The American landscape photographer, Ansel Adams, uses side aligned wide-view Oriental perspective. See *Moon Rise*, 1941. The Paris based Romanian Brassai uses side aligned wide-view, Semitic perspective, See *Dance Hall*, 1932. Since the Second World War photography has grown in importance. The Americans Robert Frank and Lee Friedlander use side aligned wide-view Semitic perspective. See Frank's *Political Rally, Chicago*, 1956 and Friedlander's *Washington*, D.C. 1962. Joel Meyerowitz uses side aligned Hellenic perspective. See *Provincetown Porch*, 1977. The amazing Diane Arbus side aligned uses wide-view Oriental perspective. See *Untitled No. 6*, 1970-71.

Modernism in Britain
Modernism in Britain is proceed by the moody art of WalterRichard Sickert. He uses side aligned Hellenic perspective. See *Ennui*, 1913, Tate

Gallery, London. Modernism in Britain is advanced by the curator and writer, Roger Fry. Most British Modern artists use standard English perspective, side aligned Semitic perspective. This is used by the early English modernist Percy Windham Lewis. See his cubist abstraction, *Composition*, 1913, Tate, Gallery, London. The sculptor Henry Moore uses side aligned fixed ego Semitic perspective. See *King and Queen*, 1952-53, Hirshhorn Museum, Washington, D.C. The Britain based American, R. B. Kitaj, uses side aligned Hellenic perspective. See *Autumn in Central Paris (After Walter Benjamin)*, 1972-3, Private Collection.

Early Modernism in the United States
Modernism in the United States is proceeded by the so called Ash Can School. Robert Henri uses side aligned Hellenic perspective. See *Laughing Child*, 1907, Whitney Museum of American Art, New York City. William Glackens uses side aligned Hellenic perspective. See *Chez Mouquin*, 1905, The Art Institute, Chicago. John Sloan uses side aligned wide view Hellenic perspective. See the *Wake of the Ferry II*, 1907, the Phillips Collection, Washington, D.C. The most modern of the group is the Post Impressionist Maurice Prendergast uses side aligned Hellenic perspective. See *Central Park*, 1905, Private Collection. The virtuoso George Bellows uses side aligned Renaissance perspective. See *Cliff Dwellers*, 1913, Los Angeles County Museum of Art.

    The first generation of American Modernists gathers around Alfred Stieglitz who exhibits European Modernism and his gallery. Some had been to Europe and saw Modernism first hand and Stieglitz shows Modern European in his gallery. The American public is made aware of and alarmed by European Modernism in 1913 at the New York City Armory Show. Work by the first generation of American Modernists works are relatively conservative but often are high in quality. Max Weber who saw Cubism first hand in Paris uses side aligned peripheral perspective. See *Chinese Restaurant*, 1915, Whitney Museum of American Art, New York City. John Marin, uses side aligned wide-view Semitic perspective. See *Lower Manhattan Composition*, 1922, Museum of Modern Art, New York City. Charles Demuth uses side aligned wide view Semitic perspective. See *I Saw the Figure Five in Gold*, 1928, Metropolitan Museum of Art, New York City. Georgia

O'Keeffe uses side aligned Oriental perspective. See *Radiator Building*, 1927, Fisk University. The abstractionist Arthur G. Dove uses side aligned fixed ego Semitic perspective. See *Nature Symbolized, No 2*, ca. 1911, The Art Institute Chicago. Marsden Hartley uses side aligned disconnected Oriental perspective. See *Portrait of a German Officer*, 1914, Metropolitan Museum of Art, New York City. Two European born American Modernist sculptors are Robert Laurent who uses center aligned peripheral perspective. See *Flame*, ca 1917, Whitney Museum of American Art, New York City and the Polish Eli Nadelman who uses side aligned Hellenic perspective. See *Man in the Open Air*, ca. 1915, Museum of Modern Art, New York City.

Dada

Dada an international phenomena is launched during World War I by a group of artists in Zurich. Spurred on by the madness of the War the Dadaists produce highly inventive works from unorthodox materials and held performances involving nonsense, music and noise. The Alsatian Jean Arp uses center aligned fixed ego Semitic perspective. See his relief, *Flower Mountain*, 1916, Foundation Arp, Colment, France. The fabric artist Sophie Taeuber uses center aligned African perspective. See *Rhythms Libres*, 1919, Kunsthaus, Zurich. Kurt Schwitter's uses side aligned wide-view Semitic perspective. See *Picture with a Light Center*, 1919, Museum of Modern Art, New York City. During the War the Dada spirit invades New York by way of European artists fleeing the war. Among them is the unique Marcel Duchamp. Duchamp uses standard French perspective, center aligned Semitic perspective for his early cubist works. See *Nude Descending a Staircase No. 2*, 1912, Philadelphia. For his *Large Glass, The Bridge Stripped Bear by Her Bachelors Even* (name is a pun on Marcel), executed in New York, 1915-23, Philadelphia Museum of Art, to escape the hand of the artist he uses center aligned Renaissance perspective. The *Large Glass* is made up of images of manufactured objects and accidentally arrived at elements placed between sheets of glass now cracked, all nonsensical. Nevertheless critics and art historians have found specific meanings in it sequence of forms.

Surrealism

Surrealism begins in Paris in the twenties and grows out of Dada. It begins with a group of writers around Andre Breton who are joined by various painters and sculptors. Surrealism is an effort to unleash the unconscious in the making of art. The unpremeditated, dreams, accidents, and free associations are used. Sigmund Freud is a great influence. Surrealism takes two directions, more abstract works that exploit suggestive, irrational forms and what Savator Dali calls "hand painted dream photographs," representational works, conservative in style, with wildly improbable subject matter. The Catalan, Joan Miro uses standard Spanish reduced scale bottom aligned Semitic perspective. See *Halequin's Concert*, 1924-5, Albright-Knox Gallery, Buffalo, New York. The Italian predecessor of Surrealism, Georgio de Chirico, uses center aligned reduced scale Renaissance perspective for his enigmatic, dream like subjects. See *Soothsayer's Recompense*, 1913, Philadelphia Museum of Art. The Catalan, Salvator Dali uses reduced scale bottom aligned fixed-ego Semitic perspective. See *Persistence of Memory*, 1931, Museum of Modern Art, New York City. The Belgium, Rene Magritte uses center aligned Renaissance perspective. See *The False Mirror*, 1928, Museum of Modern Art, New York City. The Swiss-Italian sculptor and painter, Alberto Giocometti, uses center aligned wide-view Hellenistic perspective. See *The Palace at 4 A.M.* 1932-33, Museum of Modern Art, New York City. The French, Andre Masson, uses center aligned wide-view Hellenic perspective for his semi abstract *Battles of Fishes*, 1926, Museum of Modern Art, New York City. The architect Frederich Kiesler uses side aligned wide view Semitic perspective. See *Art of the Century Gallery*, 1942, New York City. Surrealism spreads around the world and is with today.

Europe in the Twenties and Thirties

This is the time of the so called the School of Paris is at the center of the art world and artists from around the world working there. The School of Paris would include Matisse and Picasso, the Cubists, the Surrealists. The Romanian sculptor, Constantine Brancusi uses side aligned wide-view, Semitic perspective. See *Mademoiselle Pogany III*, 1931, Philadelphia Museum of Art. The Italian Anedeo Modigliani reduced scale center aligned continuous Semitic perspective. See Portrait of Chaim Soutine, National Gallery of Art Washington D.C. The Lithuanian-Jewish Chaim Soutine uses side aligned wide view Hellenic perspective. See Side of Beef, 1924-25. Abright-Knox Gallery, Buffalo, New York. The Russian-Jewish painter Marc Chagall also uses side aligned continuous Semitic perspective. See *The Green Violinist*, 1923-34, The Guggenheim Museum, New York City. Maurice Utrillo uses center aligned reduced scale Semitic perspective. See *Street in Asnieres*, 1913-15, Private Collection.

The United States During the Twenties and Thirties
This is the time of Regionalism. The work of relatively conservative American artists whose subject matter is American scenes. At this same time a number of important American Modernists emerge. Among the conservatives is Edward Hopper who uses side aligned wide view Hellenic perspective. See *Early Sunday Morning*, 1930, Whitney Museum of American Art. Thomas Hart Benton a leading Regionalist uses side aligned Semitic perspective. See his mural, *City Building*, 1930, collection of the Equitable Life Insurance Company. Anna Marry (Grandma) Moses uses side aligned wide view Hellenic perspective, forms not in space. See *Checkered House*, 1943, collection of the IBM Corporation. The photographer Walker Evens, uses side aligned view Hellenic perspective. See *Miner's Home, West Virginia*, 1935. The modernist Jacob Lawrence uses side aligned continuous Semitic perspective for his series *The Migration of the Negro*, 1920-41. See *No. 1*. the Phillips Collection, Washington D.C. The most important American Modernist is the internationally influential sculptor Alexander Calder, the inventor of the mobile. Calder uses side aligned wide view Hellenic perspective. See his mobile, *Lobster Trap and Fish Tail*, 1939, Museum of Modern Art, New York City. The Modernist Stuart Davis uses side aligned continuous Semitic perspective. See *Report from Rockport*, 1940, Metropolitan Museum of Art, New York City.

Mexico.
In the 1920's Mexican artists begin producing politically charged murals that celebrate Mexico's past including its Indian heritage. The most

famous of these artists is Diego Rivera who studies in Paris. Rivera uses side aligned continuous Semitic perspective, forms in space and spacial continuity. See his Murals, *Detroit Industry*, 1932-35, Detroit Institute of Art. Jose Orozco uses side aligned wide view Oriental perspective. See his Murals for the Darthmouth College Library, *Epic of American Civilization*, 1932-34, Hanover, New Hampshire. David Siqueiros also uses side aligned Oriental perspective. See *Scream*, 1937, Museum of Modern Art, New York City. The much admired Surrealist, Frida Kalo uses side aligned wide view Oriental perspective. See *Self Portrait Between Mexico and the United States*, 1932, Private Collection.

The Abstract Expressionists and other American Modernists
In the late forties after the Second World, there emerges in New York City a group of American artists, the Abstract Expressionists, who are inspired by European modernism and European artists and writers who came to the United States during the war and in particular the Surrealists with their interest in the use of the unconscious and the accidental in making art. Abstract Expressionism stands in marked contrast to Regionalism's conservatism. The Abstract Expressionists reject "fine art" in general, eschew traditional practice and highlight the application of paint which can be individual strokes or broad areas of color. In every case what is sought is and an emotionally charged work of art. Apparent haphazardness and spontaneity not withstanding their works are controlled by the visual ego. The Armenian Archile Gorky uses side aligned wide view peripheral perspective. See *The Liver is a Cocks Comb*, 1944, Albright-Knox Gallery, Buffalo, NY. The Dutch Willem de Kooning, uses side aligned wide view Hellenic perspective. See *Woman II*, 1953, Museum of Modern Art, New York City. Jackson Pollack uses side aligned fixed-ego Attic perspective to control his famous "drip" paintings. See *Autumn Rhythm*, 1950, Metropolitan Museum of Art, New York City. Lee Krasner uses side aligned continuous Hellenic perspective. See *Celebration*, 1959-60, Private Collection. Fanz Kline uses side aligned continuous Semitic perspective. Robert Motherwell uses side aligned wide view Hellenic perspective. See *Elegy to the Spanish Republic*, 1953, Albright-Knox Gallery, Buffalo, NY. Mark Rothko also uses side aligned wide view Hellenic perspective. See *Ochre and Red on*

Red, 1954, Pillips Collection, Washington, DC. Phillip Guston uses side aligned wide view Hellenic perspective. See *Zone*, 1953-54, Private Collection. Elaine De Kooning's uses side aligned continuous Semitic perspective, as does Grace Kritian and Joan Mitchell. See De Kooning's No. 15, 1948 Metropolitan Museum, N,Y,C, Grace Haritgans *Giftwares*, 1955, Neuberger Museum, Prchace NY and Joand Mitchel's August Rue Deguerres, 1957, Baltimore Museum of art and Joan Mitchell's *August, Rue Daguerre*, 1957, The Phillips Collection, Washington D.C. Milton Avery, uses side aligned continuous Oriental perspective. See *Swimmers and Sunbathers*, 1945, Metropolitan Museum of Art, New York City. Hellen Frankenthaller uses side aligned Oriental perspective, *Mountains and Sea*, 1952, National Gallery of Art, Washington D.C. Concurrent with Abstract Expressionism is a group of abstract sculptors. David Smith, uses side aligned fixed-ego Semitic perspective. See *Cubi, XVIII*, 1964 Boston Museum of Fine Arts. Louise Nevelson uses side aligned wide view Hellenic perspective. See *Black Chord*, 1969, Private Collection. The Japanese American, Isamu Nobuchi uses side aligned wide view Oriental perspective. See *Kouros*, 1944-45, Metropolitan Museum of Art, New York City.

Pop Art

Pop Art, a new style and apparently new aesthetic follows close on the heels of and often mocks Abstract Expressionism. Pop Art returns to representation using commercial art as a source. Much of Pop Art is sophisticated, skillfully produced, and includes insightful social commentary. The English, Richard Hamilton, a pioneer, uses side aligned Semitic perspective. See his collage *What Makes Today's Home So different, So Appealing?* 1956, Kunsthalle, Tubingen, Germany. Robert Raushenberg and Jasper Johns uses side aligned wide view Hellenic perspective. See Raushenberg's *Bed*, 1955, Museum of Modern Art, New York City and John's *Flag*, 1954-55, Museum of Modern Art, New York City. The Swedish sculptor Clause Oldenburg also uses side aligned wide-view Hellenic perspective. See *Soft Toilet*, 1966, Whitney Museum of Modern Art, New York City. The American sculptor George Segal uses side aligned Hellenic perspective. See *Cinema*, 19965, Albright-Knox Gallery, Buffalo, NY. Jim Dine uses side aligned continuous Hellenic perspective.

See *Double Isometric Self Portrait*. 1964, Whitney Museum of American Art, New York City. Larry Rivers uses side aligned continuous Hellenic perspective. See *Dutch Masters and Cigars II*, 1963, Private Collection. James Rosenquist uses side aligned Hellenic perspective. See *F111*, 1965, Private Collection. Andy Wharhol uses wide view side aligned Hellenic perspective. See his screen print, *Marilyn Monroe*, 1962. The Californian, Wayne Thiebaud, uses side aligned Hellenic perspective. See *Pie Counter*, 1963, Whitney Museum of American Art, New York City. The unique Jes uses side aligned Hellenic perspective. See *Will Wonders Never Cease?* 1962, Hirshhorn Museum, Washington, D.C.

Post Modern Architecture

Post Modern Architecture is allied with Pop Art and Post Modern art. Post Modern architecture comes out of a critique of Modern Architecture for the sake of a new more open architecture. Post Modern Architecture is inspired by popular culture, vernacular commercial architecture and even the gaudiness of Las Vegas. An essential characteristic of Post Modern Architecture is the use of peripheral perspective which replaces Modern's use of continuous Semitic perspective. Postmodern buildings are experienced as a sequence of parts allowing for the interjection or ornament, traditional motifs and even the Classical orders. Robert Venturi uses side align peripheral perspective. See *Chestnut Hill House*, 1962, PA. Other Post Modern architects using side aligned peripheral perspective are: Charles Moore, *Piazza Italia*, 1975-8, New Orleans; Peter Eisenman, *Center for the Arts*, 1983-89, Ohio State University, Columbus, Ohio; the Dutch architect and writer, Rem Koolhass, *Netherlands Dance Theater*, 1987, The Hague; the English architect Norman Foster, *Telecommunications Tower*, 1992, Barcelona; the American Robert Stern, *Pool House*, 1981-2, Lewelyn, New Jersey and the "neo cubist" Richard Ghery, *Guggenheim Museum*, 1992-7, Bilbao, Spain.

Other Post World War II European and American Art

Since World War II there are numerous important artists whose' work does not fit such categories as Abstract Expressionism, Pop Art, Minimalism or postmodern. Most use standard perspectives. An exception is the Danish abstractionist, Asper Jorn who uses center aligned fixed ego

Semitic perspective. See *Green Ballet*, 1960, Guggenheim Museum, New York City. The Italian still life painter Giorgio Morandi surprisingly as an Italian uses side aligned Semitic perspective. See *Still Life*, 1951, Kunstammlung, Dusseldorf. The American, Elsworth Kelly, uses side aligned Hellenic perspective. See *Orange and Green*, 1966, Private Collection. The Czech photographer Joseph Sudeck uses wide-view Semitic perspective, forms not in space. See The *Windows of My Studio*, 1954. The German, Deiter Roth, uses side aligned wide-view Hellenic perspective. See his silk screen, *Six Picaddilies*, 1969-70. The German Anselm Keifer uses side aligned fixed ego Renaissance perspective. See *Germany's Spiritual Heroes*, 1973, Private Collection. The Russian Nicolas de Stael used side aligned Hellenic perspective. See *Agrigente*, 1954, Museum of Contemporary Art, Los Angeles. The German George Basilitz uses side aligned Hellenic perspective. See *Torso*, 1990, Private Collection. The American portraitist Alice Neel uses side aligned Hellenic perspective. See *Portrait of Andy Warhol*, 1970, Whitney Museum of American Art, New York City. Another American using side aligned wide view Hellenic perspective is Elizabeth Murray. See *Careless Love*, 1995-6, National Gallery of Art, Washington, D.C. The Californian Richard Diebenkorn uses side aligned Hellenic perspective. See *Man and Woman in Large Room*, 1957, Hirshhorn Museum, Washington, D.C. The photographers/collagists Mike and Doug Starn, use side aligned wide view Semitic perspective. See *Double Self Portrait with Mona Lisa* (The Mona Lisa herself is of course another story, 1985-89, Boston Museum of Fine Arts. The American sculptor, Martin Puryear, uses African perspective. See *Old Male*, 1958, Philadelphia Museum of Art. Ed Rossbach the remarkable California textile artist uses side aligned wide-view Semitic perspective. See *Good Omen*, 1988-90, Farago Collection, Museum of Fine Arts, Boston.

Postmodern Art
Beginning in the second half of the twentieth century there is effort to escape the bounds imposed by perspective, by the aligned visual ego, through a critique of the past and Modern art in particular for the sake of more open, more relevant art an effort that ironically confirms the importance of the aligned visual ego. The PoMo effort to escape what

is art has taken various turns including minimalism, conceptional art, performance art, land or earth art, process art and installations. All tend to treat a work of art as an open collection of evocative parts rather than a closed system. The roots of Postmodern art lie in Modern arts break with the past while aspects of the Postmodern can be found throughout the history of art. Forerunners include Cézanne's and Picasso's use of unconventional perspectives, Dada, Marcel Duchamp, Surrealism, Abstract Expressionism and Pop Art. The Minimalists step away from the past through formal simplicity and the inclusion of natural elements which supposedly opens art to the "real" world. I find these practices visual impoverishing and only reduce meaning. Frank Stella sometimes a minimalist, uses Oriental perspective for his rectilinear compositions in what he calls as a quest for "flatness." See *Agbatana III*, 1964. Allen Memorial Gallery, Oberlin College, Oberlin Ohio. Tony Smiths works are nonaligned and I would classify as works but not works of art. See *Die*, 1962, Private Collection. Donald Judd's untitled sequences of nonaligned, iron boxes, untold 1965, Hirshhorn Musée, Washington D.C. are also non art as is Drouth Rockburne's *Drawing that Makes Itself*, 1973, Museum of Modern Art, N.Y.C. Robert Morris's Installations of elemental disconnected side aligned Oriental perspective objects are intended for particular places, but are visually unconnected with either the place or each other. See *Cloud, Boiler, Floor Beam, Table*, 1964. Installation, Green Gallery, New York City. Carl Ingres *Pieces of Work*, 1969, Rex Collection, Switzerland is made of disconnected, Semitic perspectives shapes. Saul Les Itys frontal perspective *Linear Designs on Walls*, 1970's, are disconnected, Semitic perspectives shapes that do not coherently relate to the room. Richard Sera's *One Ton Prop*, 1969, Museum of Modern Art, New York City is composed of massive side aligned Semitic perspective disconnected metal plates. Robert Smithson's side aligned Semitic perspective disconnected, earth work, *Spiral Jetty*, 1970, Great Salt Lake, Utah, is not coherently related to the lake which is part of the work. Dan Flavin's composition, *Column Installation*, 1969-70, is made of commercial disconnected light fixtures. Process Art is composed of transient events transformed by forces of nature and not the action of an artist and so not works of art although termed such. See Robert Morris's *Steam Sculpture*, 1967-73. Performance art is temporary and although there can be preparation it is not how the work is to be experienced. The result is theater without the coherence of conventional theater. See Bruce Nauman's *Self Portrait as a Fountain*, 1966-70, recorded in a photograph. Conceptual Art describes acts that may not be carried out yet are deemed to be like painting and sculpture. Here the visual ego largely disappears except for the written word and disconnected objects. It is not these but the ideas engendered that are the work. See Joseph Kosuth's *One and Three Chairs*, 1965, The Museum of Modern Art, New York City.

Postmodern Art History
Postmodern Art History continues Art History's emphasis on context, external worlds past and present surrounding artist and viewer. Context as I understand it is a dynamic, potentially limitless swirl of ideas and images that is never all knowable. Context is conveyed by language and visual works of art are understood linguistically as a collection of symbolic elements, but without a syntax. Context is understood to invade the mind of the artist, viewer, critic or art historian and being not all knowable allows them to freely choose what is to be related to a work of art. This can be political, social, economic, historical, psychological, psychiatric, gender related or all of the above or anything else. For me the relevance of context is determined by the finite world that is a work of art. Concomitant with ideas about context there is the idea that the artist and the work of art are conduits for images and ideas flowing consciously and unconsciously from an original context to the critic or historian who responds again in context to determine the meaning of the work. With this scenario the critic or historian becomes the ultimate creator. This is nonsense. A response to a work of art is not the work and if the response is based on a work incorrectly seen it is probably irrelevant. Who would rather read about the Sistine Ceiling than look at it? Unfortunately maybe an art historian? Art History's fixation on context I believe has its roots in the ling standing belief that reason and aesthetics are separate ways of thinking and that aesthetics is the inferior. This attitude privileges content over form, scholar over artist and carries with it a traditional prejudice against manual labor and a belief in the superiority of the male mind. I find that knowledge and

beauty are fundamentally linked by a common visual foundation and are not gender related. Leaving unclear what constitutes a work of art is another mistake. A work of art is a closed system controlled by the aligned visual ego and not a passage between vast, potentially endless contexts. Understanding a work of art depends on see in a the work in particular way. When visual form is neglected, misunderstood, relevant context is obscured and what is written becomes irrelevant. An aligned visual ego ordered visual world may be a defining attribute of the modern human being, Homo sapiens. While improved vision would have been of great use to our hunter gatherer ancestors our aligned vision has other advantages. The aligned visual ego orders our thoughts as it orders our vision and makes them communicable largely through language. Language is system of sounds that we experience in a imagined space governed by the visual ego. Language is composed of letters, sound, joined into words that are given meaning and combined into sentences. The visual ego is necessary to making clear, coherent, memorable words and sentences. Without coherence meaning is compromised. Language qualifies as art being governed by a particular use if the ego. The coherent communication of thought is essential to society. The link between language and the perspectives used by various early peoples. Peripheral perspective is used by the early Indo-Europeans, frontal perspective by Semitic language speakers and Oriental perspective by speakers of languages from the East. The aligned visual ego makes civilization possible.

Conclusion

Our aligned vision puts us in the visual world organizing and regularizing it so that is better reflects the real physical world. We use the same visual processes to make works of art. Nature is a great source of ideas and images, knowledge and beauty, but nature seems endless, ambiguous and contradictory. A work of art is finite. It makes a statement that in contrast to nature establishes its and our own separate being. Art like religion and science orders our world. Art is in our genes. Art defines us as human beings. Art is here to stay.

Notes

[1] The visual ego described here differs from what Ernest Mach calls the phenomenal ego and James J. Gibson the visual ego. In both cases the ego described is a visual field that includes part of the viewer seen one eye, what I call the nonaligned visual world. See James J. Gibson, The Perception of the Visual world, 1950, 27 and 225.

[2] See Brian M. Fagen, The Journey from Eden, the Peopling of Our World, 1999.

www.ingramcontent.com/pod-product-compliance
Lightning Source LLC
LaVergne TN
LVHW041543060526
838200LV00037B/1122